An Introduction to French Pronunciation

THE LIBRARY

An Introduction to French Pronunciation

Glanville Price

Basil Blackwell

Copyright © Glanville Price 1991

First published 1991

Basil Blackwell Ltd
108 Cowley Road, Oxford, OX4 1JF, UK

Basil Blackwell Inc.
3 Cambridge Center
Cambridge, Massachusetts 02142, USA

British Library Cataloguing in Publication Data

A CIP catalogue record for this book is available from the British
Library

Library of Congress Cataloging in Publication Data

Price, Glanville,
    An introduction to French pronunciation / Glanville Price.
        p.   cm.
    Includes bibliographical references.
    ISBN 0-631-15475-2 – ISBN 0-631-15476-0 (pbk.)
    1. French language – Pronunciation. I. Title.
    PC2137.P75   1991
    448.1 – dc20   90-1073
                                                        CIP

Typeset in 11 on 13 Times
by Joshua Associates Ltd., Oxford
Printed in Great Britain by
Billing and Sons Ltd, Worcester

Contents

1 General Considerations

1.1 Introduction

1.1.1 Pronunciation, by definition, is to do with a language in its spoken form, i.e. with sounds. A printed book expresses whatever it has to say, even about pronunciation, through the very different medium of the written language. So, right at the outset of a book such as this we have a problem – or, rather, a number of interrelated problems. In particular, we have to ask and, one hopes, answer the questions: what justification is there for even attempting to discuss the spoken medium through the written medium? and, secondly, supposing such justification can be demonstrated, how do we set about doing it? In the following paragraphs we shall try to answer these questions – though to some extent indirectly rather than directly.

The first thing to be made clear is that this is not a book for absolute beginners. It is a book for those who already have at least a basic knowledge of how French is pronounced but who need help and advice with a view to improving their pronunciation, to making it more authentic, to eliminating serious errors, and to reducing to an acceptable minimum features of their pronunciation that would betray them as non-native-speakers.

The use of the expression 'reducing to an acceptable minimum' in the previous paragraph is deliberate. To be realistic, one must accept that very few foreign learners of a language, even those who are linguistically gifted and who have lived for years in a country where the language in question is spoken, achieve such a degree of perfection in their pronunciation that they can pass themselves off unfailingly as native-speakers.

A more realistic ambition is to be able to pronounce the language well enough to speak confidently without feeling self-conscious about such traces of a foreign accent as will in most cases remain. A great deal of guidance can in fact be given that ought to ensure that most of the errors that so often betray one as a foreigner are avoided. That is the aim of this book.

That said, it has to be recognized that no book can, by itself, go more than a certain distance – though nevertheless a considerable distance – towards giving one 'a good accent'. To achieve the best accent one is capable of means, of course, hearing and listening to the language as it is spoken by native-speakers (and, as we shall see, there is a significant difference in the language-learning process between merely hearing the language and actually listening to it in an informed way). Ideally, this means talking 'live' to native-speakers. If for any reason that is not possible a great deal can be learned by listening to radio or television broadcasts which are now becoming increasingly available with the advent of satellite TV (though, as we shall see in 9.7.2, there are aspects of 'media French' that are not to be imitated in ordinary conversation) or by using one of the many taped courses that are on the market.

There are no tapes or cassettes to go with this book. The intention is not to provide yet more listening material but to help the reader to listen *in an informed way* to whatever sources of spoken French are available and so to derive the maximum benefit from them.

Having said earlier that no book can go more than a certain distance towards giving one a good accent, we must now stress that the same is true, if less obviously so, of spoken material. If recordings or the services of native-speakers are to be used to the best advantage, they must be supplemented by a systematic analysis of the phonetic structure, or sound-system, of the target language (i.e. the language that is being studied). This analysis will be all the more helpful if it is, at least to some extent, contrastive, i.e. if it draws attention to differences between the target language and the learner's own language. Unless they are gifted with exceptionally well-developed powers of mimicry, learners will almost certainly not be able to imitate as well as they otherwise might even a native-speaker who is physically present, much less so a disembodied recorded voice. They need to know what to listen for, what it is they are trying to imitate. Otherwise they may not even realize that what they are saying is by no means a close, let alone a perfect, imitation of what they hear. That is what this book is about. (To take a very simple example: how many English-speaking learners of French are aware that the *t* of English *too* differs in at least two important respects from the initial *t* of French *tout*? See 14.3.1 and 14.4.2.)

1.1.2   One further problem that has to be taken into account is that not all French-speakers pronounce their language in the same way. As with English or indeed any other widely spoken language, regional differences exist. There is considerable variation in pronunciation between one part of France and another, and even more so between one part of the wider French-speaking world and another. There are also differences arising out of such factors as age, educational background and social attitudes (e.g. snobbery or inverted snobbery, conformism or anti-conformism). And the pronunciation of one and the same individual may vary, and sometimes quite markedly so, depending on such factors as the formality or informality of the occasion and the speed of utterance.

The kind of pronunciation described in this book is basically the kind that educated Parisians might normally use in everyday conversation. This is not in any absolute sense 'better' than any other kind of French pronunciation but as it is the basis of French as taught in schools, colleges and universities all over the world it would be perverse not to adopt it here too. However, where there seems good cause to do so, we shall draw attention to regional, social or stylistic differences in pronunciation.

1.1.3   Just as it is impossible within one short book to describe all types of French pronunciation, or even all major varieties, so it is impossible for us, in making contrastive comments, to take account of all possible varieties of English pronunciation. Our comments on English pronunciation are therefore not necessarily applicable to all native-speakers of English. Generally speaking, the standard of comparison is what is usually known as 'Received Pronunciation' (by whom it is 'received' is not entirely clear . . .) or 'RP' – perhaps most easily, if somewhat vaguely, defined as the pronunciation of those BBC newsreaders and presenters who are not perceived as having any particular regional accent. This is not the pronunciation of most English-speakers and, to repeat the point just made in relation to French, it is not in any absolute sense 'better' than other varieties of English. But it *is* a widely recognized standard – it is, if nothing else, a useful point of reference for characterizing other types of pronunciation. We shall, however, occasionally take account of features of pronunciation that are current in other types of British English or in American English.

1.1.4   A more specific problem arises out of the fact that the ordinary spelling of French – like that of English – is at best an inadequate and imperfect way of representing the pronunciation of the language. We need a more efficient system and the one we shall adopt is that of the International Phonetic Association, the IPA – the abbreviation can also stand for International Phonetic Alphabet. Other systems are available and are often found in particular in various works on the history of the French language. But the IPA system is by far the most widely used and is the one employed in many standard works of reference, including the two best, and best-known, two-way dictionaries of French and English, viz.: *Harrap's New Standard French and English Dictionary* and *The Collins–Robert French Dictionary: French–English English–French*.

The IPA symbols used in this book and the sounds they represent are listed in 1.7 below and are discussed in some detail later (4.7–4.12, 5.1 and 6.6–6.11, and in the sections on each vowel, semi-consonant and consonant). At this stage it is enough to note that the principle on which the system is based is that, in a given language, a given sound is always represented by the same symbol and a given symbol always represents the same sound. This remark, however, calls for two comments:

(i) The word 'sound' as used above is imprecise – strictly speaking, we should use the term 'phoneme', which is discussed in 1.2 below.

(ii) The expression 'in a given language' is important; for example, French *troupe* and English *troop* can both be represented in the IPA as /trup/, but the pronunciation of the vowel and of each of the three consonants is in reality noticeably different in the two languages.

1.2 Sounds, Phonemes and Allophones

1.2.1 In print, the three letters *c*, *a* and *n* making up the word *can* are discrete units, i.e. they are quite clearly separate from one another. It is essential to grasp the idea that *this is not true of speech*. Spoken language – and this is true of all languages – does not consist of a succession of discrete units. Speech is a continuum, a process in which the speech organs (the tongue, the lips, the velum, etc. – see 2.3 to 2.5 below) are constantly moving from one position to another. This means that the pronunciation of a given 'sound' may be affected by that of preceding sounds and, even more so, by that of following sounds.

If it seems odd that the pronunciation of one sound can be

conditioned by that of a following sound, i.e. by that of a sound that has not yet been uttered, one only has to realize that, when we speak, we not only know what we are about to say but are also *anticipating* what we are about to say; consequently, the quality of any sound we utter may well be affected by the fact that we are at the same time preparing to utter a later sound. (For more on this, see chapter 18, 'Consonantal Assimilation'.)

A simple example ought to help to make this clear. Most speakers of English would assume that in words such as *keel* and *cool* the first consonant (and whether it is written as *k* or *c* is irrelevant) is the same – the IPA would represent it as /k/. But in reality, in most people's English, the /k/ of *keel* and the /k/ of *cool* differ in at least two respects. One of these is very obvious: when we start to say *keel*, the lips are spread, i.e. they take up (or are beginning to take up – it varies from speaker to speaker) the position required for the following *ee*; but, for many though not all speakers of English, when they start to say *cool*, i.e. even before they utter the /k/, the lips are to some extent rounded, i.e. they have already taken up (or are beginning to take up) the position required for the following *oo*: the lip position required for the vowel is taken up before the /k/ is uttered and, to that extent, we can say that the pronunciation of the /k/ is influenced by the fact that the speaker is anticipating the following vowel. (In French, this spreading or rounding of the lips in words such as *qui* or *coup* is even more marked.) But that is not all. The *ee* of *keel* is a front vowel, i.e. it is pronounced by raising the front of the tongue, while the *oo* of *cool* is a back vowel, i.e. it is pronounced by raising the back of the tongue. The consequence of this is that, when the tongue makes contact with the roof of the mouth, as it must when we pronounce the sound /k/, it does so further forward in the mouth for *keel* than for *cool*. This is less obvious than the anticipation of the lip-position of the vowel but it has an even greater effect on the quality of the consonant, as can easily be checked by asking somebody to pronounce the words *keel* and *cool* but to stop once they have pronounced the initial consonant – the difference is quite noticeable.

Similarly, in English as spoken in the south of England, there is a clearly audible distinction between the way /l/ is pronounced before a vowel as in *leaf*, *like*, *loose* (the so-called 'clear *l*') and the way it is pronounced after a vowel as in *feel*, *mile*, *cool* or in words such as *little*, *people*, *tackle* (the so-called 'dark *l*'). (For more on this, see 16.2 below.)

1.2.2 These distinctions between different varieties of /k/ or between different varieties of /l/ are certainly real enough, but they are of a very different order from the distinction between, say, *t* and *d*. The difference is that it is not possible in English (though it may be in other languages) to use the distinction between clear and dark *l* or between the /k/ of *keel* and the /k/ of *cool* to make meaningful distinctions, whereas this *is* possible with *t* and *d*. We have, for example, such pairs as *ten* and *den* or (in British but not necessarily in American English) *writer* and *rider*, in each of which the distinction of meaning depends solely on the distinction between *t* and *d*. Whatever the spelling may be, in pronunciation the two members of each pair are identical in other respects. But if, for the sake of argument, we were to suppose that the /k/ of *keel* was always written as a *k* and the /k/ of *cool* as a *c*, it would still be impossible in English to have a pair of words *kool* and *cool*, since the /k/ of *keel* cannot occur in English before the vowel of *cool*. In other words, the distinction between these two /k/ sounds does not have the same importance in English as that between *t* and *d*, since it depends solely upon the 'phonetic context', i.e. upon the sounds that precede or follow, and cannot be used to make meaningful distinctions. The same is true of clear and dark *l*.

Such variations in the pronunciation of what is basically the same 'sound' (to continue to use for the moment a term that is not strictly appropriate) occur in all languages, though the man or woman in the street is not generally aware of them.

1.2.3   It should now be clear why the term 'sound' is inadequate. The *t* of *ten* and the *d* of *den* are different sounds – but so are the /k/ of *keel* and the /k/ of *cool*. But whereas in the first case the difference enables us to make meaningful distinctions, in the second it serves no such purpose. We can therefore distinguish, within a given language, between what we might call *distinctive* or *functional* 'sounds' and *non-distinctive* or *non-functional* 'sounds'. The technical term for a distinctive or functional 'sound' is a **phoneme**, and the non-distinctive or non-functional varieties of each phoneme are known as **allophones**. So, in English, the phoneme /k/ has at least two allophones (in reality, there are many more), namely those of *keel* and of *cool*. Likewise, clear *l* and dark *l* are allophones of the same /l/ phoneme.

1.2.4   The number of allophones in any given language probably runs into hundreds, even within the speech of one person. The number of phonemes, however, is comparatively small. It is not possible to give a precise figure for the number of phonemes in French since the number will vary slightly depending (i) on whether or not certain sounds are counted as phonemes or as allophones of the same phoneme (see 4.9.5, 5.1.2 and 10.7.2 below), and (ii) on whose French the count is based on, since some speakers make distinctions that others do not (see 10.9.1 and 10.10.3 below). But it is probably true to say that most native-speakers of French have a repertory of from thirty-one to thirty-four phonemes. English has rather more – A. C. Gimson, for example (1970: 45 and 97), recognizes forty-four (twenty-four consonants and twenty vowels). Spanish, on the other hand, has as few as twenty-two or twenty-three phonemes, and some languages have even fewer.

1.2.5   As far as the 'sounds' of French are concerned, our task is twofold. We have first of all to identify and classify the phonemes of the language, and then to identify and describe the principal allophones of each phoneme.

Transcriptions normally take account only of phonemic differences and are given between oblique strokes, e.g. *siècle* /sjɛkl/, but when attention is specifically drawn to allophonic features such as, for example, the voiceless *l* of *siècle* (see 16.5.1), brackets are used [sjɛkl̥].

1.3 Suprasegmental Features

In addition to dividing up an utterance into its phonemes (or, more precisely, into the particular allophones representing the phonemes in the utterance in question), we also have to take account of what are known as 'suprasegmental features', i.e. features of pronunciation that relate not just to one allophone but to sequences of allophones. In particular, we have to show (i) which syllables are subject to a particular stress, and (ii) what the basic intonation patterns of French are. These topics are discussed in chapters 9 and 20.

1.4 The Articulation of French

One point that must constantly be borne in mind until it becomes second nature when speaking French is that very much greater muscular effort goes into the pronunciation of French than into that of English and that, consequently, French is pronounced with much greater tension than English. It has even been claimed more than once (see for example Carton, 1974: 42) that no other language is pronounced with comparable muscular energy and tension. However that may be in general, it is certainly true that not only English but such languages as German, Italian, Portuguese, Spanish, Russian and Welsh are pronounced with less muscular effort and tension than French. English, however, with its very relaxed pronunciation, is perhaps at the other extreme from French and it is particularly important that English-speakers should change their articulatory habits when speaking French. The effect of this tension is particularly noticeable in so far as it affects the lips, in which it can be seen that both the spreading and the rounding of the lips – for the vowels of *lit* and *loup* respectively, for instance – are much more pronounced than in the case of English.

1.5   The Organization of this Book

One problem that is faced by anyone writing a book of this kind is that of finding the most satisfactory – or, rather, the least unsatisfactory – way of organizing the material. One has to divide the material up on some basis or other and there is much to be said for, and little to be said against, starting by making the traditional and phonetically defensible distinction between vowels and consonants (while recognizing that in many languages, French being one of them, the distinction is not absolutely clear cut: see chapters 5 and 13 on the semi-consonants).

But, as we have seen (1.2.1), human speech does not consist, like letters on the printed page, of a mere succession of discrete units. Speech is a process, not a state, and the speech organs are constantly in motion, not only moving from the position they occupied for the production of an earlier sound but preparing to produce sounds that the speaker knows, if only half-consciously, that he or she is going to be uttering later in the same word or in a succeeding word. To take a couple of simple examples:

(i) The *k* sounds of words such as *keen*, *cat* and *cool* are all slightly different because of the fact that, in each case, the position of the lips and the tongue is to some extent anticipating that needed for the production of the following vowel.

(ii) The vowel of *can* is different from that of *cat* because, when we utter the vowel of the word *can*, we are already preparing to utter the following nasal consonant, *n*, and consequently some air escapes through the nose and the vowel is therefore slightly nasalized.

We are therefore forced to the conclusion that in order to understand the pronunciation of the consonants one needs to know something about the vowels, and that in order to understand the pronunciation of the vowels one needs to know something about the consonants.

There is no fully satisfactory way out of the dilemma. The solution adopted in this book is inevitably something of a compromise. We begin with three general chapters, after which we take a first, rather general, look at the vowels, the semi-consonants and the consonants. This ought to provide the reader with the basic knowledge needed in order to understand later chapters in which the vowels, semi-consonants and consonants are discussed at greater length.

Interspersed at appropriate places among the chapters on vowels, semi-consonants and consonants, or following them, are others discussing such highly important aspects of French pronunciation as the rhythmic group, the syllable, liaison and intonation.

1.6   References and Further Reading

A small selection of books that can be recommended on general phonetics or on the pronunciation of French or English is given at the end of the book under the title 'References and Further Reading'. Only works specifically referred to in this book and a few other particularly useful works currently in print are included. When reference is made to any of these in the text of the book, the 'author–date' system is used – e.g. 'Catford, 1988: 51–6' refers to J. C. Catford, *A Practical Introduction to Phonetics*, 1988, pp. 51–6.

1.7   Phonetic Symbols

1.7.1   The following IPA symbols (see 1.1.4) are used in this book:

1.7.2   Standard French:

(i) Vowels (see chapter 4):

/i/	lit	/y/	tu	/u/	fou	/ɛ̃/	vin
/e/	pré	/ø/	feu	/o/	dos	/œ̃/	un
/ɛ/	prêt	/œ/	peur	/ɔ/	botte	/ɔ̃/	bon
/a/	patte			/ɑ/	pâte	/ɑ̃/	dans
		/ə/	je				

(ii) Semi-consonants (see chapter 5):

/j/ yeux   /ɥ/ lui   /w/ ouest

(iii) Consonants (see chapter 6):

/p/	pas	/f/	fou	/r/	rouge
/b/	bas	/v/	vous	/l/	lit
/t/	tas	/s/	sou	/m/	ma
/d/	dos	/z/	zone	/n/	nous
/k/	coup	/ʃ/	chat	/ɲ/	vigne
/g/	grand	/ʒ/	jaune	/ŋ/	parking
/ʔ/	(glottal stop – see 14.6)				

1.7.3   Other languages (including Canadian French):

(i) Vowels:

/æ/ RP English cat (see 1.1.3 and 10.9.2)
/ɜ/ RP English bird (see 10.7.1)
/ɪ/ English bit, Canadian French vite (see 10.12.2)
/ʏ/ Canadian French jupe (see 10.12.2)
/ʊ/ RP English put, Canadian French toute (see 10.12.2)

(ii) Consonants:

/θ/ English thick (see 14.4.2)
/x/ Scottish loch, German Bach, Spanish hijo (see 16.1.2)
/ɣ/ Spanish pagar (see 16.1.2)

2 The Production of Speech

2.1 Introduction

Human speech involves the use of various anatomical organs whose primary purpose is connected with breathing and/or eating and drinking, or with related activities such as coughing, sneezing, spitting, biting, sucking. For our purposes, it can be assumed that the sounds of speech are produced by expelling air from the lungs and modifying or momentarily stopping its flow as it passes first up the windpipe and between the so-called 'vocal cords' (see 2.2.1) and then through the mouth and/or the nose (see figure 1).

2.2 The Vocal Cords and Voice

2.2.1   The 'vocal cords' are not in fact cords at all but two bands of muscular tissue that stretch across the larynx from front to back at the point known as the 'Adam's apple'. The term 'cords' is, however, well established and no harm will be done if we continue to use it. The cords may be kept apart from one another (except at the front where they are attached adjacent to one another) or be brought together as a kind of valve that can close off the air stream, momentarily penning in the lungs and trachea (or windpipe) the air that has been inhaled. (One can sometimes feel the effect of this in the throat when the air is retained in this way for certain kinds of muscular effort such as lifting a heavy object or defecating.) The cords may be drawn towards one another, not so much so as to block the airstream entirely but close enough for them to vibrate and produce voice (see 2.2.3). Alternatively, though this is not the place to go into detail, various types of friction at the vocal cords produce the English *h* sound or a whisper. (For further information on the various types of sound produced at the vocal cords, see for example Abercrombie, 1967: 25–8; Catford, 1988: 51–6; Gimson, 1970: 8–10.)

2.2.2   The space between the vocal cords is known as the 'glottis' and the corresponding adjective is 'glottal' (see in particular 14.6).

2.2.3   In its technical sense, 'voice' is the sound produced by rapid vibration (many times a second) of the vocal cords. It is,therefore, a musical sound, produced in a similar way to the sound produced by the vibration of the strings of a violin or a piano or the vibration of the reed of a clarinet. Each individual voice has of course a considerable range of pitch, from high to low. The explanation for this is that the vocal cords can be held in varying degrees of tension. The tenser they are, the more frequently they vibrate and, consequently, the higher the pitch.

The fundamental difference between, say, on the one hand *d* and *z* and, on the other hand, *t* and *s* is that *d* and *z* are accompanied by this vibration of the cords, i.e. by voice, whereas *t* and *s* are not. On this basis, we can divide consonants into two categories, **voiced** and **voiceless** (but see also 18.2 and 18.3). The sound of a voiceless consonant is not musical – in reality, it is just noise.

For our present purposes, it can be assumed that all vowels are voiced. (In reality, voiceless vowels can and do occur – see 10.11.)

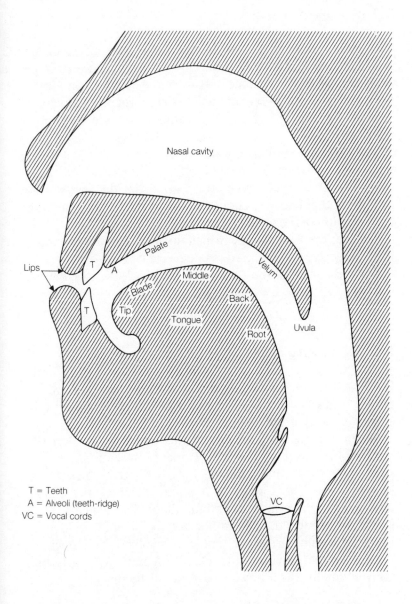

Figure 1   The speech organs (schematic diagram)

2.3   Articulators

The great variety of sounds that exist in the languages of the world are produced by the different ways in which the passage of the airstream through the oral and nasal cavities is modified by the relative positions of such speech organs – known as 'articulators' – as the tongue, the teeth, the lips and the roof of the mouth.

The production of each sound involves two articulators, at least one of which is movable. The movable articulators, otherwise known as 'active articulators', are the tongue, the lips, the soft palate (or velum) and the uvula, i.e. the rearward continuation of the velum (see 2.4.3).

The 'passive articulators', which do not move, are the teeth, the teeth-ridge and the hard palate (see 2.5).

For a diagram of the relative positions of the articulators, see figure 1.

2.4   Active Articulators

2.4.1   The most mobile of the articulators, and one which comes into play in the production of the great majority of speech-sounds, is the tongue.

When retracted into the mouth, the tongue is not a longish, flattish object as it is when it protrudes between the teeth (i.e. when one sticks one's tongue out) but much thicker and bunched up. The tongue is a highly flexible and mobile muscular organ and, in describing the way in which a given sound is produced, it is important to be able to identify precisely which part of the tongue is involved. The tongue is not, of course, divided into clearly demarcated parts but, conventionally, the following parts are distinguished:

  (i) the tip
 (ii) the blade (the part immediately behind the tip)

(iii) the middle (further back still – the term 'front' which is often used for this part of the tongue is misleading but, unfortunately, well established)
(iv) the back
 (v) the root.

2.4.2   The lips are, of course, the most visually noticeable of all the articulators and call for no further comment here.

2.4.3   As can be verified by running the tongue along the roof of the mouth, the front part – as far as about the half-way point – is hard while the back part is soft. As a technical term in phonetics, the 'palate' refers only to the front part, i.e. the hard palate. The rear part, or soft palate, is known as the 'velum' (a Latin word meaning 'veil'). As can easily be seen by looking into someone else's mouth (or, with the help of a mirror, into one's own mouth while shining a light into it), the velum ends in an appendage which is known as the uvula.

The velum (and with it, the uvula) is movable. When lowered, it allows air to escape through the nose. When raised, it blocks off the nasal passage so that air escapes only through the mouth. This can easily be seen if one opens one's mouth wide, shines a light in, looks into a mirror and first breathes in through the mouth (the velum is raised) and then breathes out through the nose (the velum is lowered). In the descriptions of French vowels and consonants in chapters 10 and 14–16 below, it should be assumed that, in the absence of any indication to the contrary (as in the case of nasal vowels, 10.10, and nasal consonants, 16.3), the velum is raised.

2.5   Passive Articulators

2.5.1   The teeth need no explanation.

2.5.2   The teeth-ridge, otherwise – and very frequently in works on phonetics – known as the alveoli or alveolar ridge, is the ridge, very easily felt with the tongue or a finger, immediately behind the upper teeth; it could equally well be considered as the front edge of the hard palate.

2.5.3   As mentioned above (2.4.3), 'palate' as a term of phonetics refers only to the hard palate.

2.6   Terminology

2.6.1   It is convenient to have a set of adjectives to refer to the various articulators; the following (all of them derived from Latin) are in common use in works on phonetics:

Name of articulator	Corresponding adjective
tongue	lingual
lip(s)	labial
velum	velar
uvula	uvular
teeth	dental
teeth-ridge (alveoli)	alveolar
palate	palatal

2.6.2   With reference to sounds for which the tongue is an active articulator, it is usual to use the adjective corresponding only to the other articulator, e.g. a /k/ that is pronounced by raising the tongue until it makes contact with the velum (see 14.4.3) is generally referred to as **velar** rather than **linguo-velar** (which, strictly speaking, would be more accurate). But when the tongue is not involved, reference is made to both articulators, in particular in the use of the term **bilabial** for /p/ and /b/ which are pronounced with both lips (see 14.4.1), and **labio-dental** for /f/ and /v/ which have the lower lip as an active articulator and the top teeth as a passive articulator (see 15.3.1).

3 The Articulation of French

3.1 Articulatory Tension

3.1.1 The first general distinction to be noted between the pronunciation of English and that of French is that French is characterized by much greater muscular tension. This has important consequences for the pronunciation both of vowels and of consonants. In particular:

3.1.2 Whereas in English the lips are relatively relaxed, in French they are much tenser; this is very noticeable in the fact that, when the lips are spread, particularly for the vowel /i/ (as in words such as *dit*, *vite*, *grise*), the corners of the mouth are stretched apart much more vigorously than in the case of the English vowel of such words as *tea*, *meet*, *please*, while they are much more decisively rounded and thrust forward for the vowel of French *coup*, *toute*, *rouge*, etc., than for the vowel of English *coo*, *toot*, *spoon*, etc.

3.2 Pure Vowels

The fact that the lower jaw does not move when a French vowel is being pronounced means that its quality remains steady throughout, i.e. French vowels are 'pure' and have none of the fluctuation in quality that characterizes southern

English vowels (though not necessarily the vowels of English as spoken with, say, a northern English or a Scottish or Welsh accent). What happens in southern English, and also in American English, is that, as a result of a generally relaxed type of articulation, the lower jaw tends to close when one is pronouncing the vowel of, for example, words such as *day*, *date*, *gaze* or *go*, *toe*, *slow*, *rope*, *close*. The fact that the mouth is less open for the latter part of the -*a*- or the -*o*- than at the start means that the quality of the sound changes. In reality, then, the vowels are not 'pure' – they are, in fact, diphthongs, and just as much so as the diphthongs of words such as *boy*, *oil* or *cow*, *town*, *house*.

4   The Vowel Phonemes

4.1   Principles of Classification

If we are to classify the vowel phonemes of a language on a systematic basis, we need to lay down the factors that have to be taken into account. For French (though not necessarily for other languages, where fewer, more or different factors may come into the picture), there are four relevant factors, viz.:

  (i)   the point of articulation (see 4.2)
 (ii)   the height of the tongue or, alternatively, the degree of aperture (see 4.3)
(iii)   lip configuration (see 4.4)
(iv)   orality or nasality (see 4.5)

4.2   Point of Articulation

'Point of articulation' is merely the technical term for 'the place in the mouth where a sound is produced'. French vowels may be classified, broadly speaking, according to whether they are pronounced in the front of the mouth, i.e. between the blade of the tongue and the palate, or between the back of the tongue and the velum. We may therefore speak of 'front vowels' and 'back vowels'. (Many languages also have 'central' vowels but we do not need this category for our present purposes.)

4.3   The Height of the Tongue or the Degree of Aperture

This factor can best be explained by taking an example. The French vowel /a/ as in *ma*, *patte*, etc., is pronounced in the front of the mouth with the tongue hardly raised at all and the mouth fairly wide open. The vowel /i/ as in *lit*, *vite*, etc., is also a front vowel, but pronounced with the tongue raised well up towards the palate and the mouth only slightly open. Depending on whether we choose to base our terminology on the height of the tongue or on the degree of aperture (i.e. openness) of the mouth, we can refer to the vowel /i/ either as a **high front vowel** or as a **close front vowel** and to /a/ either as a **low front vowel** or as an **open front vowel**. In between, as we shall see (10.6), there are two other vowels, namely the *é* of *été*, etc. (high-mid, or half close) and the *è*, *ê* of *très*, *bête*, etc. (low-mid, or half open). (The terms 'half close' and 'half open' should not be taken too literally; strictly speaking, they refer respectively to vowels that are 'rather less than half open' and 'rather more than half open', but the terms 'half close' and 'half open' are convenient and in such widespread use that it would be pedantic to reject them.)

4.4   Lip Configuration

In referring, for example, to /i/ as a high front vowel we have not in fact described it adequately, as the same description applies to the sound represented in French as *u*, as in *du*, *lutte*, *mur* (see 10.3). The difference lies in the fact that the *i* of *lit*, etc., is pronounced with the lips spread and the *u* of *mur*, etc., with the lips rounded. We can therefore distinguish between the two by saying that *lit* has a **high front unrounded** (or **spread**) vowel and *mur* a **high front rounded** vowel.

We shall see (chapter 10) that, of the sixteen French vowels that we shall identify, eleven are rounded. And, in this connection, it should be remembered that the rounding of the lips in French is appreciably more pronounced than it is for approximately similar vowels in English.

4.5   Orality or Nasality

In describing most European languages, we should not need to take account of this factor (except perhaps to mention that, before a nasal consonant such as *n*, some air may escape through the nose while the preceding vowel is being uttered – this can happen in English in words such as *can*, etc., in which case we have a slightly nasalized allophone of the vowel). Certain languages, however, French being one of them (others are Portuguese and Polish), have vowels in which the velum is lowered throughout, allowing the airstream to escape freely through the nose as well as the mouth, and which therefore have a pronounced nasal quality. French has four such vowels, those of words such as *vin*, *un*, *son*, *grand* (see 10.10), which are not allophones of other phonemes but phonemes in their own right.

4.6   Classification and IPA Symbols

In 4.7–4.11, we are concerned mainly with the classification of the vowel phonemes and with the IPA symbols that represent them. The individual vowels are discussed in greater detail in chapters 10 and 11.

4.7   Front Unrounded Vowels

The front unrounded vowels and the IPA symbols for them are:

Symbol	Definition	Examples
i	high	lit, vite, dire, y
e	high-mid	été, pré, chanter, nez, j'ai
ɛ	low-mid	très, bête, jette, faire
a	low	la, patte, page

Some problems connected with the distinction between /e/ and /ɛ/ are discussed in 10.6 below.

4.8   Front Rounded Vowels

Symbol	Definition	Examples
y	high	du, lutte, mur
ø	high-mid	peu, feu, neutre, joyeuse
œ	low-mid	fleur, seul, sœur

Some problems connected with the distinction between /ø/ and /œ/ are discussed in 10.7 below.

4.9   Mute *e*

4.9.1   The term 'mute *e*' (in French, '*e* muet') refers to the vowel of *ce*, *je*, *le*, *ne*, *que*, etc., and the first vowel of *celui*, *crever*, *depuis*, *premier*, etc. It is otherwise known as 'neutral *e*' or, in French, '*e* caduc', '*e* instable' or '*e* féminin'. None of these terms is wholly satisfactory and the only reason we retain that of 'mute *e*' (which refers to the fact that, in circumstances to be discussed in chapter 11, it is not pronounced) is that it is probably the most widely used in English.

4.9.2   The symbol for mute *e* is [ə]. Its pronunciation varies somewhat from one individual to another but, generally speaking, it is a mid front vowel pronounced – and this is an important point to be borne in mind – *with rounded lips*. It is, therefore, pronounced in the same general area as [ø] or [œ] (see also 4.9.5).

4.9.3   Except in the first syllables of the words *faisan* 'pheasant' and related words, in *monsieur* and in parts of the verb *faire* (*faisant*, nous *faisons*, je *faisais*, etc.), it is always written *e*.

4.9.4   There are numerous and complex problems associated with the vowel /ə/, some of which we shall not go into.

However, the conditions in which it is or is not pronounced constitute one of the major problems in French phonetics and we therefore devote a chapter (see chapter 11) to this particular problem.

4.9.5 Another problem associated with /ə/ is that of its phonemic status. There is a case for considering that it is not in fact a phoneme but merely an allophone of /ø/ or of /œ/. For practical purposes, however, it seems simpler to consider it as an independent phoneme. (For more on this, see 11.1.1.)

4.10   Back Rounded Vowels

Note that French has no back unrounded vowels.

Symbol	Definition	Examples
u	high	coup, soupe, rouge
o	high-mid	dos, grosse, côte, autre, beau
ɔ	low-mid	folle, fort, bosse
ɑ	low	pas, pâte, grasse

Some problems connected with the distinction between /o/ and /ɔ/ are discussed in 10.8 below. On /a/ and /ɑ/, see 10.9 below.

4.11   Nasal Vowels

Symbol	Definition	Examples
ɛ̃	mid front unrounded	vin, plein, sainte
œ̃	mid front rounded	un, brun, humble
ɔ̃	mid back rounded	on, dont, long, monte
ɑ̃	low back rounded	an, grand, cent, entre

4.12   Summary Table

The vowel phonemes of French are, therefore, the following:

4.12.1   Oral

	Front unrounded	*Front rounded*	*Back rounded*
High	i	y	u
High-mid	e	ø	o
Low-mid	ɛ	œ ə	ɔ
Low	a		ɑ

4.12.2   Nasal

	Front unrounded	*Front rounded*	*Back rounded*
Mid	ɛ̃	œ̃	ɔ̃
Low			ɑ̃

5 The Semi-Consonants

5.1 General

5.1.1 French has three 'sounds' (whether they are phonemes or allophones is discussed briefly below, 5.1.2) that do not fall clearly into the category either of vowels or of consonants. Two of these correspond approximately to (though they are not totally identical with) the English *w* of *was*, *wet*, etc., and the English *y* of *yes*, *you*, *layer*, *toy*, etc. The third (see 5.1.4) has no equivalent in English or indeed in most other languages.

The three sounds in question are pronounced by raising the tongue even higher than for the three high vowels /i/, /y/ and /u/, but not so high as to cause the degree of friction characterizing fricative consonants (see 6.7) such as /f/, /v/, /s/, /z/, etc.

5.1.2 We can therefore consider the three sounds in question as **semi-consonants** corresponding to the three high vowels and assign to each its own symbol. There are, in fact, strong arguments in favour of the view that they should be classified not as phonemes but as semi-consonantal allophones of the vowels /i/, /y/ and /u/. However, for our immediate practical purposes it is more convenient to treat them as phonemes.

5.1.3 Corresponding to the vowel /i/, we have the semi-consonant represented by the IPA symbol /j/ (derived from the German value of *j* as in *Jung, ja* – it is important not to confuse this IPA value of /j/ with the *j* (= IPA ʒ) of normal French orthography, as in *je, jour*). In normal French orthography this is represented by *y*, as in *yeux* /jø/, *payer* /peje/, or by *i*, as in *pied* /pje/, or by *ll, il* or *ill* as in *fille* /fij/, *œil* /œj/, *paille* /paj/.

This is the only one of the three semi-consonants that can occur between vowels (as in *payer*) or after a vowel (as in *fille, œil*, etc.). In reality, the degree of friction is less in these circumstances than when it precedes a vowel (as in *yeux, pied*). This means that it is closer to being a consonant in words like *yeux, pied*, etc., than in words like *payer, fille*, etc. For this reason, some analyses of French make a terminological distinction between the /j/ of *yeux, pied*, etc., which is referred to as a 'semi-consonant', and that of *payer, fille*, etc., which is referred to as a 'semi-vowel'. This distinction is a valid one but it is unnecessary for our purposes and we shall therefore refer to /j/, wherever it occurs, as a semi-consonant.

5.1.4 Corresponding to the vowel /y/, we have the semi-consonant represented by the IPA symbol /ɥ/ and, in normal French orthography, by the *u* of such words as *lui, nuit, muet*. For more on this sound, which often causes considerable problems for foreigners, see 13.5.

5.1.5 Corresponding to the vowel /u/, we have the semi-consonant /w/, represented by the *ou* of such words as *oui, ouest*. It occurs particularly frequently in the context *oi* (or *oî, oy*), pronounced /wa/, e.g. *moi, voile, boîte, moyen*, or, in some words, /wɑ/, e.g. *bois, froid, mois, trois, voix*.

6 The Consonant Phonemes

6.1 Principles of Classification

As in the case of the vowels (see 4.1), before we can classify the consonants of French systematically we have to determine what factors are relevant. In practice, for French (and, indeed, for most other western European languages), the factors to be taken into account are the following:

  (i) the point of articulation (see 6.2)
 (ii) the manner (or mode) of articulation (see 6.3)
(iii) the presence or absence of voice (see 6.4).

6.2 Point of Articulation

6.2.1 Two points of articulation do not involve the tongue:

 (i) the lips
(ii) the top teeth and the bottom lip.

6.2.2 All others involve the use of the tongue as an active articulator (see 2.4.1):

(iii) the top teeth (when the other articulator is not the bottom lip)
(iv) the teeth-ridge

(v) the palate
(vi) the velum
(vii) the uvula.

6.3   Manner (or Mode) of Articulation

6.3.1   The airstream may be stopped at some point and then released, thereby producing an 'explosion', as in the case of *p*, *b* (for which the point of articulation is the lips) or of *k*, *g* (for which the point of articulation is the velum). These consonants are known as **stops** (or, alternatively, as **plosives**).

6.3.2   The airstream may not be totally blocked but forced through a narrow passage, e.g. between the tongue and the teeth as in the case of English *th* of *thick*, or between the top teeth and the lower lip as in the case of *f*, *v*, thereby causing audible friction. These consonants are known as **fricatives**.

6.3.3   The airstream may be partially blocked when the tip of the tongue is placed against the teeth or the teeth-ridge but allowed to escape around the sides of the tongue; this is the case of the various *l*-sounds that occur in French and English and which, because the air escapes around the sides of the tongue, are known as **laterals**.

6.3.4   The flow of the airstream through the mouth may be blocked at some point but the velum and uvula are lowered (see 16.3) and, in consequence, the airstream is allowed to escape through the nose. This is most noticeably the case when the point of articulation is the lips (i.e. the mouth is closed at the lips) for the consonant *m*. These consonants are known as **nasals**.

6.3.5   Given the great variety of *r*-sounds that exist in French, and the fact that they have different manners of articulation, they are temporarily left out of account here but will be discussed at some length in 16.1.

6.4   Presence or Absence of Voice

6.4.1   Voice is the sound caused by the vibration of the vocal cords (see 2.2) and consonants may be produced with or without such vibration. Consonants pronounced with this vibration, such as *d*, *z*, *l*, *m*, are known as voiced consonants. Consonants pronounced without the vibration, such as *t*, *s*, are known as voiceless consonants.

6.4.2   The fact that voice, whether accompanying a consonant or a vowel, has resonance, means that the 'carrying power' of a voiced consonant is greater than that of a voiceless consonant. This is to some extent compensated for in many languages by pronouncing voiceless consonants with greater energy and breath than voiced consonants, as is quite obvious if one compares the strength with which one articulates the voiceless initial consonants of, say, *fat* or *seal* with that of the voiced initial consonants of *vat* or *zeal*. The technical terms for these two types of articulation are **fortis** (the Latin for 'strong') and **lenis** (the Latin for 'weak'). We can therefore say that the initial consonants of *fat*, *seal*, *ten*, *pack*, etc., are **voiceless** and **fortis**, whereas those of *vat*, *zeal*, *den*, *back*, etc., are **voiced** and **lenis**.

6.4.3   However, though the features 'voiceless' and 'fortis', on the one hand, and the features 'voiced' and 'lenis', on the other, normally go together, it is possible in certain circumstances for them to be dissociated. In particular, as far as French is concerned, there are circumstances in which we can have consonants that are voiceless but lenis – what, in non-technical terms, we might call a 'voiceless *b*' etc. (see 18.2.2–18.2.4). We also, but less frequently, find voiced fortis consonants (18.2.5).

6.4.4   An important difference between French and English is that in French, except in the kinds of phonetic context referred to in 6.4.3, what are called voiced consonants really are fully voiced, whereas in English voiced stops and fricatives may be only partially voiced. By 'partially voiced' we mean that the vocal cords vibrate, i.e. voice is produced, during only part of the time it takes to utter a given consonant.

What happens in English is that, in words beginning with a voiced stop or fricative, such as *boy*, *day*, *gone*, *vain*, *zeal*, the vocal cords start to vibrate a fraction of a second after the initial consonant starts being pronounced, which means that the first part of the *b*, *d*, *g*, *v* or *z* is voiceless. When these consonants occur at the end of a word, however, the vocal cords may stop vibrating before the consonant has been completed, i.e. in words such as *rob*, *fad*, *fig*, *leave*, *maze*, the last part of the *b*, *d*, *g*, *v* or *z* is voiceless.

In French, on the other hand, the voiced consonants are *fully voiced throughout*. The difference may not be very audible to the ear of an English-speaker but is likely to be very perceptible to a French-speaker. Given that, say, initial and final English *b*, *d* and *z* are somewhere in between the French *b* and *p*, *d* and *t*, *z* and *s* respectively, a French-speaker could interpret them as representing his or her voiceless rather than voiced phonemes, e.g. *boue*, *ride*, *chose*, with the voiced consonants pronounced as in English, might sound to a French ear like *poux*, *rite*, *chausse*.

The solution for the English-speaker, until one gets to the stage of automatically pronouncing French voiced consonants correctly, is to make a conscious effort to pronounce the consonants in question as they are pronounced between vowels in English (where they are in any case fully voiced), e.g. like the *b*, *d*, *g*, *v*, *z* of *above*, *leader*, *dagger*, *living*, *razor*, or the *-s-* of *pleasure* (for which the phonetic symbol is /ʒ/ – see 6.7.2 (ii)).

6.5   Classification and IPA Symbols

In 6.6–6.11 we are concerned with the classification of the consonant phonemes of French on the basis of the factors discussed in 6.1–6.4, and with the IPA symbols that represent them. The individual consonants are discussed in greater detail in chapters 14–16.

6.6   Stops

6.6.1   The words *peur*, *patte*, etc., and *beurre*, *bon*, etc., begin with a voiceless and a voiced bilabial stop respectively, the symbols for which are /p/ and /b/.

6.6.2   The words *tout*, *tel*, etc., and *doux*, *dans*, etc., begin with a voiceless and a voiced dental stop respectively, the symbols for which are /t/ and /d/.

6.6.3   The words *car*, *quatre*, etc., and *goût*, *grand*, etc., begin with a voiceless and a voiced velar stop respectively, the symbols for which are /k/ and /g/.

6.7   Fricatives

6.7.1   The words *fils*, *fort*, etc., and *vin*, *vous*, etc., begin with a voiceless and a voiced labio-dental stop respectively, the symbols for which are /f/ and /v/.

6.7.2   French has two pairs of fricatives pronounced in the region of the alveolar ridge, namely:
   (i)   the voiceless initial consonant of *sa*, *soupe*, *cent*, etc., IPA symbol /s/, and its voiced equivalent, the initial consonant of *zéro*, etc., which in fact occurs much more frequently written as an -*s*- between vowels, as in *maison*, *oser*, *phrase*, etc., IPA symbol /z/;
   (ii)   a pair corresponding approximately (but see 15.3.3) to English *sh* as in *shoe* and to -*s*- as in *pleasure*, namely the voiceless consonants written in French as *ch*, as in *chou*, *chambre*, *chercher*, etc., IPA symbol /ʃ/, and the voiced

equivalent written as *j*, as in *je*, *jouer*, etc., or, not infrequently, before *e*, *i* or *y*, as *g*, as in *geler*, *gilet*, *gymnaste*, IPA symbol /ʒ/.

6.8   Lateral

The symbol for the one (voiced) lateral consonant of French, the *l* of *lit*, *malade*, *pâle*, etc., is /l/.

6.9   Nasals

6.9.1   French has four nasal consonant phonemes, all of them usually voiced though, as we shall see (16.6), a voiceless allophone of /m/ occurs.

6.9.2   The bilabial nasal of *ma*, *aimer*, *plume*: IPA /m/.

6.9.3   The dental nasal of *nous*, *venir*, *lune*: IPA /n/.

6.9.4   The palatal nasal, always written *gn*, as in *signer*, *vigne*: IPA /ɲ/. There is no corresponding phoneme in English – see 16.3.3.

6.9.5   A velar nasal that, as a phoneme, is always written *ng* and occurs only in words in -*ing* borrowed from English, e.g. *parking*, *meeting*, and in the word for the Austrian unit of currency, *schilling*: IPA /ŋ/. (In addition, it can occur as an allophone of /g/ in some contexts – see 18.3.4.)

6.10   *r*-Sounds

There are at least three clearly distinguishable ways (more if one counts minor variations) of pronouncing the French *r* of words such as *rouge*, *Paris*, *cher* (see 16.1). Each has its own

IPA symbol but, as for our purposes we need only one symbol, we shall follow the IPA recommendation of choosing the most convenient, which is /r/.

6.11   Summary Table

If, provisionally, we classify /r/ as a velar fricative, we can tabulate the French consonant phonemes as in table 6.1. Where there are two symbols in the same box, the one on the left represents a voiceless phoneme, the one on the right a voiced phoneme; where there is only one symbol, it normally represents a voiced phoneme.

Table 6.1 French consonant phonemes

	Point of articulation			
Manner of articulation	*Bilabial or labio-dental*	*Dental or alveolar*	*Post-alveolar or palatal*	*Velar*
Stop	p b	t d		k g
Fricative	f v	s z	ʃ ʒ	r
Lateral		l		
Nasal	m	n	ɲ	ŋ

7 The Rhythmic Group

7.1 Introduction

Any act of speech, whether it is, on the one hand, no more than a one-syllable utterance such as 'Stop!' or 'Yes' or, on the other hand, a protracted lecture or speech, lasts for a finite and measurable length of time. It is equally obvious that one-word utterances such as 'Stop!' or 'Sorry!' cannot be subdivided (except into their constituent phonemes, or also, in the case of 'Sorry!', 'Impossible!', etc., into syllables), but that many longer utterances *can* be subdivided on some basis or other. What is far less clear, however, is precisely how an utterance of some length is to be subdivided.

For the sake of argument, let us assume that an utterance consists of one or more sentences and that the problem we have to address is that of subdividing the sentence. This assumption in fact oversimplifies things somewhat, as even the division of an utterance into sentences is not without its difficulties – but that need not concern us here. A more serious problem arises when we attempt to subdivide the sentence.

7.2 The Different Types of Group

7.2.1 The problem is very considerably complicated by the fact that we could take into account at least three different types of subdivision, each of which would produce what we shall call 'groups', and that the groups arrived at on one basis may or may not coincide with those arrived at on one or more of the other bases. In what follows, we shall choose relatively simple examples for the sake of clarity. Our definitions of the three types of group, arrived at on the basis of different approaches, are deliberately left somewhat vague – any attempt to be rigorously precise would take us into very deep waters, and in any case is not necessary for our purposes.

7.2.2   The **breath group** corresponds to everything that is said between two intakes of breath; in fact, the breath group could be longer than the sentence, as in 'Come tomorrow. I'll be glad to see you', if spoken without taking a breath between 'tomorrow' and 'I'll'.

7.2.3   The **sense group** can be taken, for our purposes, as corresponding to grammatical subdivisions within the sentence – but there could well be differences of opinion as to where these fall: for example, while there could be little doubt that the sentence 'Every Saturday morning, provided it's not raining, he goes swimming' consists of three sense groups, there could well be a measure of disagreement as to how many groups, up to a maximum of five, a sentence like 'He takes the children for a swim in the town pool every Saturday during the holidays' falls into. What is quite clear, however, is that there are very frequently, though not of course by any means always, a number of sense groups within the same breath group.

7.2.4   The **rhythmic group** is, as we shall see (7.3), of particular importance for French, whereas, for English or many other languages, an analysis based on breath groups and sense groups alone might well suffice.

7.3   The Rhythmic Group

7.3.1   In what follows, | is used to indicate a division between rhythmic groups (note that this is not a standard IPA symbol).

7.3.2   No complete set of hard-and-fast rules for dividing a sentence into rhythmic groups can be given, but the following indications should provide adequate guidance:

(i)   The rhythmic group may or may not be followed by a pause.

(ii)   Wherever there *is* any kind of normal pause between breath groups and/or sense groups, there is a division between rhythmic groups (pauses for hesitation, as in *Je vous ai . . . euh . . . sousestimé*, are excluded from this definition).

(iii)   The rhythmic group coincides with one or more sense groups.

(iv)   Constructions such as the following can never be split, i.e. they *must* fall within the same rhythmic group:

(a)   preposition + noun phrase, pronoun, infinitive, etc., e.g. *pendant quelques instants*, *avant de partir*;

(b)   adjective + following noun, e.g. *cette agréable surprise*, *une charmante petite fille* (but adjectives following the noun *may* – but not necessarily – form a different rhythmic group, e.g. *c'est un étudiant | très intelligent*, *il a des problèmes | insurmontables*);

(c)   subject and object pronouns and their verb, e.g. *je vous les donne*, *envoyez-le-moi* (but a noun subject or object *may* – but not necessarily – form a separate rhythmic group, e.g. *mon fils aîné | arrive demain* or *ils écrivent | plusieurs lettres*);

(d)   auxiliary verb + past participle, e.g. *nous avons fini*, *(mon frère) est parti*, *(mon frère) sera choqué*.

7.3.3   The rhythmic groups are quite short – usually only three or four syllables and rarely more than seven syllables. So, for example, while *mon frère arrive* would normally be treated as one group and *mon frère arrive demain* might or might not be divided (with a division before or after *arrive*), it is highly likely that the following only slightly longer utterances would be divided as indicated: *mon frère aîné | arrive demain*, *mon frère arrive | demain matin*; likewise, while *il fait*

froid chez vous (and even *il fait toujours froid chez vous*)
would normally constitute a single rhythmic group, the
sentence *il fait toujours froid | dans votre pays* would be
divided.

7.3.4 Another factor to be taken into consideration is the
speed of utterance: in general, the more slowly one is speaking,
the greater the number of rhythmic groups in a given sentence,
e.g. an expression such as *en hiver et en été*, which could well
constitute a single group in fairly rapid speech, would be
divided (*en hiver | et en été*) in slower speech. But even in a
slow, and even formal, delivery one would be unlikely to subdivide short utterances such as *mon frère arrive*, *que faites-
vous là?*, *il travaille toujours*.

7.3.5 In the following examples, | indicates a necessary or
highly probable division, and a space an optional division (it is
unlikely that divisions would be made at any other points):

> *Personne ne comprend| ce que vous dites*
> *Je peux vous prêter | cinquante francs*
> *Demain | je pars pour Paris*
> *Les enfants | sont partis en vacances | au bord de la mer*
> *Mon cousin   travaille toujours*
> *C'est un enfant   difficile*
> *Venez me voir | jeudi   ou vendredi*
> *Jean   a beaucoup voyagé | en France   et en Espagne*
> *C'est Pierre   qui a écrit | l'article dont tu parles*.

7.4   The Rhythmic Group and the Word

So far, we have said nothing about the importance of the word
as a possible subdivision of the group – and the reason for that
is that, in French, the word has no importance as a phonetic
unit. If, for example, one hears a phrase in French that one
does not understand, there are no phonetic criteria by which

one can tell where one word ends and another begins: there is no phonetically identifiable unit between the syllable (see chapter 8) and the rhythmic group. Phonetically speaking, one can say that in French the word does not exist: what is important is not the word but the rhythmic group, as we shall see in relation to:

   (i) syllabic division – the final consonant of one word may belong phonetically to the first syllable of the following word (see 8.3)

 (ii) the position of stress – French has group-stress not word-stress (see 9.4)

(iii) the pronunciation of mute *e* (chapter 11)

(iv) intonation (chapter 20).

8 The Syllable

8.1 Introduction

8.1.1 The way in which French words – or, more precisely, French utterances (see 8.3) – are divided into syllables may seem a purely theoretical question. However, as we shall see, it has a number of important practical applications relating to such matters as stress (9.4), the distinctions between /e/ and /ɛ/ (10.6), between /ø/ and /œ/ (10.7) and between /o/ and /ɔ/ (10.8), and vowel length (chapter 12). It is therefore important to grasp the principles of French syllabification.

8.1.2 Throughout this section it must always be borne in mind that we are dealing with *pronunciation, not spelling*. Note in particular that:

(i) There is no final consonant in words such as *lit* /li/, *doux* /du/, *grand* /grɑ̃/.

(ii) There is only one consonant in between the vowels of words such as *donner* /dɔne/, (*nous*) *battons* /batɔ̃/.

(iii) Digraphs such as *ch* /ʃ/, *ph* /f/, *th* /t/, *gn* /ɲ/ represent single consonants, as in *cacher* /kaʃe/, *éléphant* /elefɑ̃/, *télépathie* /telepati/, *agneau* /aɲo/.

(iv) A single written consonant, *x*, represents a succession of two pronounced consonants in words such as *vexer* /vɛkse/, *examen* /ɛgzamɛ̃/.

(v) There is no nasal consonant in words such as *chanter*

/ʃɑ̃te/, *emprunter* /ɑ̃prœ̃te/, *bonté* /bɔ̃te/, *intention* /ɛ̃tɑ̃sjɔ̃/, (*nous*) *tombons* /tɔ̃bɔ̃/ – in each case, the *n* or the *m* merely indicates that the preceding vowel is nasalized.

8.1.3   For our present purpose, we shall indicate the division between syllables by a hyphen, e.g. *téléphoner* /te-le-fɔ-ne/, *partir* /par-tir/, but it should be noted that this is not a standard IPA convention.

8.2   The Rules of Syllabification

The rules for dividing French utterances into syllables are basically quite simple. They are as follows:

(i)   An initial consonant, cluster (i.e. a succession of two or more consonants) or semi-consonant necessarily belongs to the following syllable, e.g. the /b/ of *beau* /bo/, the /pl/ of *plein* /plɛ̃/, the /tr/ of *trou* /tru/, the /j/ of *yeux* /jø/, the /p/ of *pied* /pje/, the /m/ of *moi* /mwa/.

(ii)   A final consonant or cluster necessarily belongs to the preceding syllable, e.g. the /k/ of *sac* /sak/, the /ʃ/ of *bouche* /buʃ/, the /tr/ of *litre* /litr/ (but see 8.3 below).

(iii)   A single consonant or semi-consonant between vowels belongs to the following syllable, e.g. *chanter* /ʃɑ̃-te/, *heureux* /œ-rø/, *difficile* /di-fi-sil/, *radical* /ra-di-kal/, *loyal* /lwa-jal/, *mouiller* /mu-je/; this applies even across word-boundaries within the same rhythmic group (see 8.3).

(iv)   Apart from the exceptions noted in (v) below, a pair of consonants occurring between vowels is split, i.e. the first belongs to the preceding syllable and the second to the following syllable, e.g. *partie* /par-ti/, *vexer* /vɛk-se/, *acné* /ak-ne/, *altitude* /al-ti-tyd/, *capsule* /kap-syl/. Note that for this purpose a semi-consonant does *not* count as the equivalent of a consonant, i.e. a single consonant followed by a semi-consonant belongs to the following syllable, e.g. *nation* /na-sjɔ̃/, *situer* /si-tɥe/, *Savoie* /sa-vwa/.

(v)   A cluster consisting of a stop, /f/ or /v/ + /r/ or /l/ is not split and belongs to the following syllable, e.g. *patrie* /pa-tri/, *détruit* /de-trɥi/, *tendrement* /tã-drə-mã/, *compris* /kɔ̃-pri/, *secret* /səkrɛ/, *aigrette* /ɛ-grɛt/, *complet* /kɔ̃-plɛ/, *doubler* /du-ble/, *râcler* /rɑ-kle/, *beuglant* /bø-glã/, *souffrant* /su-frã/, *livraison* /li-vrɛ-zɔ̃/, *gonfler* /gɔ̃-fle/.

(vi) Most intervocalic groups of three consonants can be divided on the basis of (iii) and (iv) above, e.g. *portrait* /pɔr-trɛ/, *construit* /kɔ̃s-trɥi/. Others, all of them having /s/ as the middle consonant, and occasional examples where /s/ is the second of four consonants, are usually considered to be divided thus: *abstinent* /ap-sti-nã/, *substitut* /syp-sti-ty/, *abstrait* /ap-strɛ/ (for the pronunciation of *b* as /p/, see 18.2.4), but for practical purposes the matter is of no importance since, even if the division were taken as /aps-trɛ/, etc., the preceding syllable would still be closed (see 8.4).

8.3 Syllabification within the Sense Group

As is explained in chapter 7, the basic phonetic unit, in French, is for many purposes not the word but the rhythmic group. The principles of syllabification outlined in 8.2 apply within the group, with the result that a consonant whose corresponding written form comes at the end of one word belongs phonetically to the initial syllable of a following word beginning with a vowel and falling within the same group, e.g. *les grands hommes* /le-grã-zɔm/, *nous avons trop à faire ici* /nu-za-vɔ̃-tro-pa-fɛ-ri-si/.

8.4 Closed and Open Syllables

A syllable ending in a consonant (i.e. which is 'closed' by a consonant) is known as a **closed syllable** (e.g. the first syllable of *partie* /par-ti/, the second syllable of *public* /py-blik/ and both syllables of *certaine* /sɛr-tɛn/). A syllable ending in a vowel is known as an **open syllable** (e.g. the second syllable of *partie* /par-ti/, the first syllable of *public* /py-blik/ and both syllables of *chanter* /ʃɑ̃-te/).

8.5   Syllable-Timing and Stress-Timing

An important characteristic of French is that, however rapidly or however slowly one is speaking, each syllable, regardless of whether or not it is stressed (see chapter 9), takes up approximately the same amount of time: there is, as Abercrombie (1967: 98) puts it, 'a constant rate of syllable-succession'. French is, therefore, what is known as a 'syllable-timed language' whereas English is a 'stress-timed language' in which intervals between stressed syllables are more or less equal and, consequently, syllables will take up more or less time depending on how many of them there are between two successive stresses. More generally, it seems on the basis of present knowledge that all languages fall into one or other of these categories and that the great majority of European languages are, like English, stress-timed; among the relatively few syllable-timed European languages, apart from French, are Basque, Finnish and Hungarian.

9 Stress

9.1 Normal Stress

9.1.1 In many languages, some syllables are given a greater degree of stress than others, i.e. greater prominence as a consequence of being pronounced with greater energy. This can easily be illustrated from such English words as *ordinarily*, *beautiful*, where the stress is on the first syllable (*ord-*, *beau-*), *reception*, *behaviourism*, where it is on the second syllable (*-cep-*, *-hav-*), *disappointment*, where it is on the third (*-point*), or *Americanese*, where it is on the fifth and last syllable (*-ese*). (These comments relate to the main stress of a word – there are also other degrees of stress, in particular the secondary stress of the first syllable, *dis-*, of *disappointment* and of the second syllable, *-mer-*, of *Americanese*, but this need not concern us here.)

9.1.2 The rules governing the position of the main stress in the word vary considerably from one language to another. The position may be relatively fixed, as in German, where the stress on most (though not all) words is on the first syllable, or Welsh, where the stress in most words is on the last syllable but one. On the other hand, the position of the stress in English, as is illustrated by the examples given in 9.1.1, is very variable. But in all these languages, and in most other European languages, the main stress is associated with the individual word. To take English again as our starting point, the main stress on the word *beautiful* is always on the first syllable and the main stress on *behaviour* is always on the second syllable, regardless of their position in the sentence.

9.1.3   The situation in relation to French is very different in that the normal stress is associated not with the word but with the rhythmic group (see chapter 7). (For the distinction between normal stress and emphatic stress, see 9.2.1.) To anticipate a point that will be fully developed in 9.4, we can say that in *la petite maison* the only normally stressed syllable is *-son*, while in *la maison est petite* the only normally stressed syllable is *-tite*.

9.1.4   There is no universally recognized terminology for referring to different types of stress. In particular, what is here referred to as 'normal stress' is elsewhere variously termed 'unemphatic stress', 'tonic stress', 'final stress', 'grammatical stress' and 'logical stress' (the least satisfactory of the lot).

9.2   Emphatic Stress

9.2.1   It frequently occurs in English, and in other languages that have the normal stress on a fixed syllable, that that syllable is given an even greater degree of prominence, i.e. is pronounced with even more energy than normally, as one way of expressing some kind of emotion or reaction, e.g. surprise, indignation, anger, pleasure, terror, relief, disgust, admiration, or for some other expressive purpose such as uttering a request or a warning. This can be illustrated by such sentences as the following, in which the stressed syllable is printed in bold type:

*What a **wonderful** view!*
*He's gone and bought a **harp**sichord!*
***Stu**pid!*
*I've **seen** him!*

He's fantastically clever!
Please *don't forget!*
Take that disgusting thing away!

We shall refer to this particular type of stress as **emphatic stress**. Again anticipating what is to come later (9.5), we merely note here that, while French also has an emphatic stress, it functions very differently from its counterpart in English. Whereas, as we have seen, this kind of emphasis is expressed in English by giving the normally stressed syllable extra prominence, in French emphatic stress usually falls on a different syllable from the normal stress.

9.2.2 'Emphatic stress' is often known in French as an 'accent affectif' or, more usually, as one type of 'accent d'insistance', the other type being the contrastive stress.

9.3 Contrastive Stress

A greater than normal degree of stress may also be given to a word not in order to express an emotion or reaction as in the case of emphatic stress but in order to highlight the meaning it expresses and, in particular, to draw a contrast with some other word or concept, expressed or unexpressed, e.g.:

*I didn't **write** to him, I **tel**ephoned*
*They live in **Man**chester not **Birm**ingham*
*I bought a **dic**tionary* (and, by implication, not something else that I might have bought).

This we shall call **contrastive stress**.

So far, there may not seem to be much difference between contrastive stress and emphatic stress. The difference emerges clearly, however, in such utterances as *I said 'de**cep**tion' not 're**cep**tion'* or *They live in **North**ampton not **South**ampton*, in which the stress falls on a syllable other than the one that takes the normal stress.

Contrastive stress in French is discussed in 9.6.

9.4   Normal Stress in French

9.4.1   Normal stress in French always falls on the last syllable of the rhythmic group (see chapter 7). It has to be added immediately that, when one listens to French, this may not be the impression one gets: the reason for this is that other kinds of stress are so widely used as to overshadow the normal stress. Furthermore, the normal stress is relatively weak in French, both as compared with other Romance languages such as Italian and Spanish (and even more so as compared with English or German) and as compared with emphatic and contrastive stress. For this reason, foreigners whose own language has a relatively strong normal stress should take care, when speaking French, not only to stress the correct syllable but also not to overstress it. The normal stress in French, though real, is in fact barely perceptible.

9.4.2   Normal stress is indicated in phonetic script by placing ['] before the stressed syllable. The same convention can also be used for our present purposes in normal orthography, e.g.:

Je pars de'main	/ʒə par də'mɛ̃/
Où va-'t-il?	/u va'til/
C'est une belle mai'son	/sɛt yn bɛl mɛ'zɔ̃/

Longer utterances consisting of more than one rhythmic group will, of course, have a normal stress on the last syllable of each group, e.g.:

Les en'fants| sont partis en va'cances| au bord de la 'mer
lez ɑ̃'fɑ̃ | sɔ̃ parti ɑ̃ va'kɑːs | o bɔr də la 'mɛːr

Mon frère aî'né| a beaucoup voya'gé| en Es'pagne
mɔ̃ frɛr e'ne | a boku vwaja'ʒe | ɑ̃n ɛs'paɲ
|et dans le Midi de la 'France
|e dɑ̃l midi dla 'frɑ̃ːs

9.4.3   The fact that normal stress falls only on the last syllable in the rhythmic group means that the same syllable in the same word is sometimes stressed and sometimes not, depending on its position in the utterance, e.g. *je l'ai* '*vu* | *pendant les va'cances* /le va'kɑːs/, but *les vacances d'é'té* /le vakɑ̃s de'te/. As we shall see (12.2–12.7), this is a factor of crucial importance in determining whether or not a vowel is long.

9.4.4 We have seen (8.5) that French is a syllable-timed language, i.e. that each syllable, whatever its degree of stress, takes up more or less the same amount of time, whereas English is a stress-timed language. This means (to take an example from Abercrombie, 1967: 97) that in an English utterance such as '*which is the* '*train for* '*Crewe,* '*please?* the stressed syllables (1 – *which*, 2 – *train*, 3 – *Crewe*, 4 – *please*) are equally spaced out and, in consequence, that the two-syllable phrase *for Crewe* and the three-syllable phrase *is the train* each get the same amount of time as (and correspondingly less time per syllable than) the monosyllabic phrases *which* and *please*. In a syllable-timed French sentence, however, the intervals between normally stressed syllables will be irregular, since such syllables may be separated by any number of equally timed but unstressed syllables up to (normally) a maximum of six or seven (see 7.3.3).

9.5   Emphatic Stress in French

9.5.1 In English, emphatic stress is effected by giving even greater prominence to the syllable that bears the normal stress, i.e. by pronouncing it with even greater energy than normally. In French, this is not the case. In French, emphatic stress in most cases affects the first syllable, though if this begins with a vowel it frequently falls on the second syllable (which, in most such cases, begins with a consonant, though there are a very few words, such as *ahurissant* /a-y-ri-sɑ̃/, in which the first two syllables both begin with a vowel). Emphatic stress can be indicated by the mark ["] before the syllable concerned, e.g.:

(i) Emphatic stress on the first syllable:
C'est un château magnifique /sɛ tœ̃ ʃa'to ‖maɲi'fik/
Fermez la porte /‖ferme la 'pɔrt/
Il fait beau ce soir /il fɛ ‖bo sə 'swa:r/
Je n'ai jamais dit ça! /ʒə ne ‖ʒame di 'sa/

(ii) Emphatic stress on the second syllable:
J'ai un problème insoluble /ʒe œ̃ prɔblɛm ɛ̃‖sɔ'lybl/
Ce dictionnaire | est tout à fait indispensable /sə diksjɔ'nɛ:r |
ɛ tut a fɛ ɛ̃‖dispɑ̃'sabl/
Quelle idée ahurissante! /kɛl ide a‖yri'sɑ̃:t/

9.5.2 The emphatic stress can, however, fall on the initial
syllable even if it begins with a vowel, particularly in utterances
of an exclamatory nature, e.g. *"absolu'ment!* /‖apsɔly'mɑ̃/,
"impo'ssible! /‖ɛpɔ'sibl/, *"ouvrez la 'porte!* /‖uvre la 'pɔrt/,
"attendez-'moi! /‖atɑ̃de'mwa/, *"incroy'able!* /‖ɛkrwa'jabl/.
In a sense, the exception is often apparent rather than real, in
that, in such cases, the syllable taking the emphatic stress
begins with a glottal stop (see 14.6), e.g. [‖ʔapsɔly'mɑ̃], which
serves the same function as an initial consonant.

In other cases, a liaison consonant carried over from the preceding word (see chapter 19) serves as the 'consonne
d'insistance', e.g. *c'es"t impo'ssible!* /sɛ ‖tɛ̃pɔ'sibl/, *troi"s
énormes ca'mions* /trwa ‖zenɔrm ka'mjɔ̃/, *se"s innombrables
en'fants* /se ‖zinɔ̃brablə zɑ̃'fɑ̃/, *que"l imbé'cile!* /kɛ ‖lɛ̃be'sil/.

9.5.3 Two additional features to be noted in relation to
emphatic stress are:
(i) that the stressed syllable is pronounced at a higher pitch
than would otherwise be the case
(ii) that the initial consonant is frequently lengthened, i.e. its
articulation is prolonged; this added length can be indicated in
phonetic script by a colon, e.g. *quelle "belle mai'son!* [kɛl ‖b:ɛl
mɛ'zɔ̃], *"magni'fique!* [‖m:aɲi'fik], *j'ai "trop de tra'vail* [ʒe
‖t:ro d tra'vaj], *in"dispensable* [ɛ̃ ‖d:ispɑ̃'sabl].

9.5.4 An utterance such as *c'est impossible!* can therefore, in terms of emphatic stress, be pronounced (even not allowing for cases where the consonant is not lengthened) in at least three ways, viz. [sɛt ɛ̃"pːɔ'sibl], [sɛt "ʔɛ̃pɔ'sibl], [sɛ"tːɛ̃pɔ'sibl].

9.5.5 It should be noted that the use of an emphatic stress is not something exceptional: a high proportion of rhythmic groups have one in ordinary speech. Furthermore, the emphatic stress is appreciably stronger than the normal stress which, as we have seen (9.4.1), is relatively weak in French as compared with English and many other languages. Consequently, it is emphatic stress rather than normal stress that a foreigner – especially if he or she has a relatively strong normal stress in his or her own language – is particularly likely to notice when listening to French.

9.6 Contrastive Stress in French

9.6.1 The simplest type of contrastive stress (which we also indicate by ["]) is that in which there is an explicit contrast between syllables, each of which is stressed, e.g.:

> *Il n'arrive pas mardi, il arrive jeudi*
> /il nariv pɑ "mar'di, il ariv "ʒø'di/
> *Vous avez dit 'réception' ou 'déception'?*
> /vuz ave 'di "resɛp'sjɔ̃ u "desɛp'sjɔ̃/

In the case of final syllables of a rhythmic group, this means giving added stress to the normally stressed syllable, e.g.:

> *Il est francophile* | *plutôt que francophobe*
> /il ɛ frãko"fil | plyto k frãko"fɔb/.

9.6.2 Where there is no overt phonetic contrast (as in the cases dealt with in 9.6.1) but a contrast between two phonetically unrelated words or, rather, between the ideas they express, this is often indicated by intensifying the stress on the normally stressed syllable, e.g.:

Je dirais│ qu'il est étourdi│ plutôt que malveillant
/ʒə di'rɛ│ kil ɛt etur"di   │ plyto k malvɛ"jã/

Such a contrast is often implicit rather than explicit, e.g. *Je l'ai
rencontré │ à Bordeaux* /ʒə le rãkɔ'tre│a bɔr"do/ 'I met him at
Bordeaux [i.e., by implication, not somewhere other than
Bordeaux]'.

9.7 Other Types of Stress

9.7.1 The above observations (9.4–9.6) do not claim to be
anything like exhaustive. A thorough-going discussion of the
different types of stress in French is beyond the scope of this
book. Indeed, such a discussion would perhaps not be fully
possible in the present state of our knowledge: those who *have*
tackled the problem in some detail are not always in total
agreement and it appears that there is scope for further
research on the subject.

9.7.2 One type of stress in particular that has not been
referred to above but which must be mentioned, if only to
warn the reader against using it in ordinary conversation, is
that sometimes known as *l'accent démarcatif* or *l'accent
didactique*. This is often heard in reading aloud or in various
forms of public address (lectures, speeches, news bulletins,
etc.), and it consists of stressing the first syllable of a rhythmic
group, even when the word or syllable itself (which may be, for
example, an article or a preposition) is not such as ever to take
a normal stress. Carton states (1974: 119): 'Nous avons relevé
des centaines d'exemples d'insistance sur des syllabes initiales
de syntagmes ("*de* son côté, *la* conférence . . .").' This kind of
stress pattern is a frequent feature of the French of radio and
television newsreaders and presenters but it *should not be
imitated* in conversational usage.

10 The Vowels in Detail

10.1 Introduction

10.1.1 Note that all French vowels are pronounced with *much greater muscular tension and vigour* than English vowels (see 3.1) and that they are *pure vowels, never diphthongized* (see 3.2).

10.1.2 In certain circumstances, stressed vowels (see 10.1.3) are long. This topic is dealt with fully in chapter 12. For the moment, all that is necessary is to note that a colon after a vowel indicates that it is long, e.g. *mur* /myːr/, *monde* /mɔ̃ːd/.

10.1.3 For the purposes of this chapter, it will be assumed that the last syllable of a word that can be stressed *is* stressed and that all other syllables are unstressed. In reality, the situation is rather more complex (see chapter 9), but the complications do not invalidate the data and rules given in this chapter.

10.1.4 For convenience, we shall discuss the vowels in the following order:

(i) the three high vowels (i, y, u) (10.2–10.4);
(ii) the three pairs of mid-vowels (e/ɛ, ø/œ, o/ɔ) (10.5–10.8);

(iii) the low vowels (a, ɑ) (10.9);
(iv) the nasal vowels (ɛ̃, œ̃, ɔ̃, ɑ̃) (10.10).

As mute *e* (ə) is in many respects in a category of its own and poses so many problems, it is treated in a chapter of its own (chapter 11).

10.2 /i/ – High Front Unrounded

The main point to observe is that this is a much more spread vowel than that of English *see*, *meat*, etc., i.e. *the corners of the lips are pulled much further apart than in English*.

/i/ is usually written *i*, e.g. *lit* /li/, *vite* /vit/, *livre* /liːvr/, but occasionally *î*, e.g. *gîte* /ʒit/, *ï*, e.g. *naïf* /naif/, or *y*, e.g. *y* /i/, *psychique* /psiʃik/, *Yves* /iːv/.

Note that in words such as *iodine*, *lion*, the *i* is not a vowel but the semi-consonant /j/ (/jɔdin/, /ljɔ̃/) – on the alternation between /i/ and /j/, see 13.7.

10.3 /y/ – High Front Rounded

English has no corresponding vowel – and, indeed, no front rounded vowels at all. This does not mean that such vowels are 'difficult' for English-speakers (millions of whom, doubtless, have learned to pronounce them correctly), but only that they are unfamiliar and need special attention.

For the correct pronunciation of /y/, the tongue position is virtually the same as for /i/, but the lips are protruded and very clearly rounded (as for /u/ – see 10.4). In other words, try and say a French /i/ while maintaining the lip-position for French /u/.

/y/ is always written *u* or *û*, e.g. *tu* /ty/, *lune* /lyn/, *mur* /myːr/, *dû* /dy/.

A frequent fault on the part of English-speakers, who do not have a high front rounded vowel in their own speech, is to attempt to produce some kind of substitute for /y/ by beginning with a front unrounded vowel ([i]) and continuing with a back rounded one ([u]), i.e. something like [liun] (or [liwn]) for /lyn/; this may or may not be intelligible to a French-speaker but, at best, will mark the speaker out as having a strong foreign accent.

For the alternation between /y/ and /ɥ/, see 13.7.

10.4 /u/ – High Back Rounded

The main point for English-speakers to note is that, for French /u/, the lips are clearly and firmly (not, as in English, loosely) protruded and rounded.

English-speakers from areas (e.g. parts of Lancashire and central Scotland – but see below) where the *oo* of *too*, *cool*, etc., is centralized (i.e. pronounced further forward in the mouth than in other varieties of English) should take particular care to pronounce /u/ well back in the mouth; there is all the more need to stress this point since there seems to be a growing tendency on the part of speakers from many parts of England to bring the vowel somewhat forward, though not as much so as in the areas mentioned above.

It should also be noted that many English-speakers start rounding their lips some time *after* beginning to pronounce the vowel of *too*, *cool*, *food*, *loo*, etc., thereby producing something like [təu, kəul, fəud, ləu]. In French, on the other hand, in words such as *tout*, *coup*, *loup*, etc., the lips are rounded, and firmly so, *even before the consonant is pronounced.*

/u/ is nearly always written *ou* or *oû*, e.g. *loup* /lu/, *foule* /ful/, *ouvre* /u:vr/, *goût* /gu/. Note, however, the words *où* /u/, *août* /u/ or /ut/, and *saoûl* /su/ (and its derivatives).

For the alternation between /u/ and /w/, see 13.7.

10.5   The Three Pairs of Mid-Vowels

In discussing each of the pairs e/ɛ, ø/œ and o/ɔ, we shall need to distinguish (i) between stressed positions and unstressed positions (see chapter 9) and (ii) between open and closed syllables (see 8.4).

10.6   /e/ – High-Mid Front Unrounded; /ɛ/ – Low-Mid Front Unrounded

10.6.1   The main problem here is to know when to pronounce /e/ and when to pronounce /ɛ/. As we shall see, there is a tendency to pronounce /ɛ/ in closed syllables and /e/ in open syllables.

10.6.2   In closed syllables, either stressed or unstressed, the distinction between /e/ and /ɛ/ does not arise: the pronunciation, whatever the spelling (*e, è, ê, ai, ei*, etc.), is /ɛ/ (which may or may not be long – see 12.6–12.8), e.g.:

(i) stressed syllables: *sec* /sɛk/, *lettre* /lɛtr/, *sèche* /sɛʃ/, (*il*) *achète* /aʃɛt/, *fête* /fɛt/, (*vous*) *faites* /fɛt/, *pleine* /plɛn/, *lèvre* /lɛːvr/, *chaise* /ʃɛːz/, *beige* /bɛːʒ/

(ii) unstressed syllables: *festival* /fɛstival/, *question* /kɛstjɔ̃/, *esprit* /ɛspri/, *serpent* /sɛrpɑ̃/, (*il*) *lèvera* /lɛvra/, (il) *aimera* /ɛmra/. This applies even when the spelling is *é*, e.g. *événement* /evɛnmɑ̃/, *sécheresse* /sɛʃrɛs/, *pécheresse* /pɛʃrɛs/ (though /seʃrɛs/, /peʃrɛs/ are also possible). Note however that *élever* /elve/ and its derivatives *élevage* /elvaːʒ/, etc., normally have /e/. See also 10.6.5 (iv).

Note that, though *j'ai* is /ʒe/, *ai-je* must, in accordance with the above rule, have the vowel /ɛ/, e.g. *Quels droits ai-je?* /kɛl drwa ɛːʒ/.

10.6.3   In open stressed syllables, the pronunciation is either /e/ or /ɛ/, depending on the word.

The pronunciation /e/ occurs in the following circumstances:

(i) when the spelling is *é* (including *ée*, *és* and *ées*), *er* or *ez*, e.g. *chanté(e)(s)*, *chanter*, *chantez* /ʃãte/, *pré* /pre/, *chaussée* /ʃose/, *léger* /leʒe/, *nez* /ne/

(ii) in the words *pied* /pje/, and *clef* (also spelt *clé*) /kle/

(iii) in the verb ending -*ai*, e.g. (*je*) *finirai* /finire/, (*je*) *mangeai* /mãʒe/

(iv) in the words *quai* /ke/, and *gai* /ge/.

Elsewhere, the pronunciation is /ɛ/, notably:

(v) when the spelling is *e*, *è* or *ê* followed by one or more consonants, except as indicated in (i) above, e.g. *sujet* /syʒɛ/, *billet* /bijɛ/, (*je*) *mets*, (*il*) *met* /mɛ/, *aspect* /aspɛ/, *est* /ɛ/, *après* /aprɛ/, *prêt* /prɛ/

(vi) when the spelling is *ai*, *aî*, except as indicated in (iii) and (iv) above, e.g. *balai* /balɛ/, *vrai* /vrɛ/, *mai* /mɛ/, (*je*) *sais*, (*il*) *sait* /sɛ/, (*je*) *fais*, (*il*) *fait* /fɛ/, (*je*) *vais* /vɛ/, (*je*) *disais*, (*elle*) *disait*, (*ils*) *disaient* /dizɛ/, (*je*) *finirais*, (*elle*) *finirait* /finirɛ/, *français* /frãsɛ/, *laid*, *lait* /lɛ/, *s'il vous plaît* /silvuplɛ/, *jamais* /ʒamɛ/.

If the above 'rules' are followed, then we have pairs differentiated only by the distinction /e/ ~ /ɛ/ (~ = 'contrasting with'), such as *pré* /pre/ ~ *prêt* /prɛ/ and the following:

/e/		/ɛ/	
poignée	/pwaɲe/	*poignet*	/pwaɲɛ/
jouer	/ʒwe/	*jouais, jouet*	/ʒwɛ/
fée	/fe/	*fait*	/fɛ/
aller, allée	/ale/	*allais, allait*	/alɛ/
gai, gué	/ge/	*guet*	/gɛ/

Note however that there is a widespread and increasing tendency for /e/ to be substituted for /ɛ/ in stressed open syllables, e.g. (to take up some of the words listed under (v) and (vi) above) *billet* /bije/, *après* /apre/, *balai* /bale/, (*je*) *sais* /se/, (*je*) *disais* /dize/, *français* /frãse/. This means, among other things, that the first person singular of the conditional, e.g. (*je*) *dirais*, is pronounced in exactly the same way as the future, (*je*) *dirai* /dire/.

10.6.4 In so far as there is a distinction between /e/ and /ɛ/ in unstressed open syllables (see 10.6.5), it can be expressed as follows:

(i) where a corresponding stressed syllable has /e/ and there is no difference in spelling, use /e/, e.g.:

Stressed syllable		Unstressed open syllable	
forcé	/fɔrse/	*forcément*	/fɔrsemɑ̃/
fée	/fe/	*féerique*	/ferik/
pied	/pje/	*pied-à-terre*	/pjetatɛːr/
gai	/ge/	*gaité* /gete/, *gaiment* /gemɑ̃/	

(ii) where a corresponding stressed syllable has /ɛ/ and there is no difference in spelling (the distinction between *ai* and *aî* can be ignored), use /ɛ/, e.g.:

Stressed syllable		Unstressed open syllable	
coquet	/kɔkɛ/	*coquetterie*	/kɔkɛtri/
mettre	/mɛtr/	(*nous*) *mettons*	/mɛtɔ̃/
prêt	/prɛ/	*prêteur*	/prɛtœːr/
pêche	/pɛʃ/	*pêcheur*	/pɛʃœːr/
(*je*) *professe*	/prɔfɛs/	*professeur*	/prɔfɛsœːr/
		profession	/prɔfɛsjɔ̃/
(*ils*) *plaisent*	/plɛːz/	(*nous*) *plaisons*	/plɛzɔ̃/
		plaisanterie	/plɛzɑ̃tri/
(*je*) *laisse*	/lɛs/	(*nous*) *laissons*	/lɛsɔ̃/
laid	/lɛ/	*laideur*	/lɛdœːr/
maître	/mɛtr/	*maîtresse*	/mɛtrɛs/
neige	/nɛːʒ/	(*il*) *neigeait*	/nɛʒɛ/

(iii) where there is no such corresponding stressed syllable, the following guidelines cover the great majority of cases (no account is taken here of *e* = /ə/ – see chapter 11):

/e/ if the spelling is *e* (for some exceptions, see below), or *é*, e.g. *message* /mesaːʒ/, *effort* /efɔːr/, *essai* /esɛ/, *descendre* /desɑ̃ːdr/, *pellicule* /pelikyl/, *léger* /leʒe/, *régler* /regle/ (as

contrasted with *règle* /rɛgl/); this also applies to the determiners *les*, *des*, *mes*, *tes*, *ses*, *ces*, and to the pronoun *les*, e.g.
les hommes /lez ɔm/, *des chats* /de ʃa/, *mes enfants* /mez
ãfã/, *ces fruits* /se frɥi/, *je les vois* /ʒə le vwa/

/ɛ/ in the verb forms *es*, *est*, e.g. *tu n'es pas beau* /ty nɛ pa
bo/, *il est là* /il ɛ la/ and before *-rr-*, e.g. *aberrant* /abɛrã/,
terrible /tɛribl/, *terreur* /tɛrœ:r/, *perroquet* /pɛrɔkɛ/,
derrière /dɛrjɛ:r/, *erroné* /ɛrɔne/ (/ɛ/ may also sometimes be
heard in some words before *-ll-*, pronounced /l/, or *-ss-*, e.g.
tellurique /tɛlyrik/, *essai* /ɛsɛ/)

/ɛ/ elsewhere, e.g. *maison* /mɛzɔ̃/, *faisceau* /fɛso/,
meilleur /mɛjœ:r/.

10.6.5 The following alternative pronunciations should be
noted:

(i) Despite what has been said in 10.6.4, it must be noted
that there is a widespread tendency, in open unstressed
vowels, to use instead of either /e/ or /ɛ/ an intermediate
vowel (known in French as *e moyen*), i.e. a vowel whose
degree of aperture is between those of /e/ and /ɛ/; this can be
represented by the symbol [ɛ̞] (a stop under the symbol for a
vowel indicates a relatively close variety); e.g.:

instead of /e/: *défend* [dɛ̞fã], *effort* [ɛ̞fɔ:r], *présence*
[prɛ̞zã:s], *téléphone* [tɛ̞lɛ̞fɔn]; this also applies to the determiners *les*, *des*, *mes*, *tes*, *ses* and *ces*, e.g. *les hommes* [lɛ̞ zɔm],
des fruits [dɛ̞ frɥi], *mes amis* [mɛ̞z ami]

instead of /ɛ/: *embêtant* [ãbɛ̞tã], *pêcher* [pɛ̞ʃe], *prêter*
[prɛ̞te], *maison* [mɛ̞zɔ̃]; this also applies to the verb forms (*tu*)
es and (*il*, *elle*) *est*, e.g. *tu n'es pas beau* [ty nɛ̞ pa bo], *il est là* [il
ɛ̞ la].

(ii) Furthermore, many speakers sometimes or always even
use /e/ instead of *e moyen* in words which, under 10.6.4,
would otherwise have /ɛ/, e.g. *pêcheur* /peʃœ:r/, *profession*
/prɔfesjɔ̃/, *laideur* /ledœ:r/, *prêter* /prete/, *maison* /mezɔ̃/,
aimer /eme/, *baiser* /beze/, *aider* /ede/, *cesser* /sese/, *neiger*
/neʒe/, *meilleur* /mejœ:r/, *terrible* /teribl/, *erroné* /erone/,
perroquet /peroke/, *tu n'es pas beau* /ty ne pa bo/, *il est là* /il

e la/; this pronunciation is particularly common with *c'est* /se/.

(iii) This is particularly so before stressed /i/ or /y/ – i.e. the vowel is raised to /e/ in anticipation of the following high vowel, e.g.:

Stressed /ɛ/	Unstressed /e/
aigre /ɛgr/	*aigrir* /egriːr/
bête /bɛt/	*bêtise* /betiːz/
tête /tɛt/	*têtu* /tety/

– likewise colloquial *vêtir, vêtu* /vetiːr, vety/ beside more formal /vɛtiːr, vɛty/ and stressed (*il*) *vêt* /vɛ/ and (except that there is no corresponding stressed /ɛ/), *aigu* /egy/. This phenomenon (which applies only to the pair /ɛ/ ~ /e/) is sometimes referred to as *vowel harmony* (or, in French, *l'harmonisation vocalique*). The term is sometimes extended to cover the pronunciation of unstressed *ê* or *ai* as /e/ in open syllables before a following /e/, as in *prêter* /prete/, etc.; there is some justification for this in the fact that, though /e/ also occurs elsewhere, as in *pêcheur* /peʃœːr/ (see above), the use of /e/ rather than /ɛ/ is more widespread in forms such as *aimer, blesser, cesser,* than in forms such as *aimable, blessant,* (*nous*) *cessons*.

(iv) There is also a tendency, though a less widespread one than those referred to under (i) and (ii) above, to use *e moyen* or /e/ in closed unstressed syllables (see 10.6.2 (ii)), when the closing consonant is /s/, e.g. *bestiaux* /bɛstjo, bestjo/, *destin* /dɛstɛ̃, destɛ̃/, *espoir* /ɛspwaːr, espwaːr/, *festival* /fɛstival, festival/, *question* /kɛstjɔ̃, kestjɔ̃/.

10.7   /ø/ – High-Mid Front Rounded; /œ/ – Low-Mid Front Rounded

10.7.1   As in the case of /y/ (see 10.3), the problem for English-speakers is that English has no front rounded vowels. Consequently, many English-speakers tend – perhaps un-

consciously – to substitute for /ø/ and /œ/ what seems to
them to be the nearest English equivalent, namely the vowel of
bird, *earn*, etc., as pronounced in those varieties of British
English where no trace of the *r* remains (so this does *not* apply
to English as spoken in south-west England, parts of Lancashire, Scotland, Ireland or North America). (The symbol for
this is /ɜ/, e.g. *bird* /bɜːd/, *earn* /ɜːn/.) The way round this is
to keep the tongue position much as for /e/ and /ɛ/ while
firmly rounding the lips as for /o/ and /ɔ/ (see 10.8): this
should, at the very least, produce sounds close enough to /ø/
and /œ/ to be easily perfected by a little fine-tuning with the
help of a native-speaker.

10.7.2 It is in fact debatable whether /ø/ and /œ/ should
not be considered as allophones of the same phoneme rather
than as separate phonemes since the number of 'minimal pairs'
(i.e. pairs of words distinguished *only* by the distinction
between these two sounds) is limited to two, viz:

> *veule* /vøːl/ 'feeble (character)' ~ (*ils*) *veulent* /vœl/ '(they)
> wish'
> (*le*) *jeûne* /ʒøːn/ 'fast' ~ *jeune* /ʒœn/ 'young'.

Furthermore, (i) *veule* and *jeûne* are not commonly used
words, (ii) there would be no likelihood of confusion between
veule (adjective) and *veulent* (verb) or between *jeûne* (noun)
and *jeune* (adjective), and (iii) in any case, some speakers do
not observe the difference but pronounce *veule* and *jeûne* like
veulent and *jeune*.

However, purely on grounds of convenience, the two
sounds are here treated as phonemes.

With the exception of *jeûne* and of a few borrowings from
English (e.g. *club* /klœb/, *pub* /pœb/, *brushing* /brœʃiŋ/),
the spelling is always *eu*, *œ* or *œu*.

10.7.3 As in the case of /e/ and /ɛ/ (10.6), we shall
distinguish between stressed and unstressed syllables and, in
each case, between closed and open syllables.

10.7.4   In closed stressed syllables, the following guidelines apply:

(i) In syllables closed by /z/, the pronunciation is /ø/ (which, in these circumstances, is long), e.g. *creuse* /krø:z/, *chanteuse* /ʃɑ̃tø:z/

(ii) With a very few exceptions (see (iii) below), other closed stressed syllables have /œ/, e.g. *seul* /sœl/, *bœuf* /bœf/, *meurtre* /mœrtr/, *aveugle* /avœgl/, *club* /klœb/, *feuille* /fœj/, *œil* /œj/, *meuble* /mœbl/, *peuple* /pœpl/, (*ils*) *peuvent* /pœ:v/, *peur* /pœ:r/, *neuf* /nœf/, *porteur* /pɔrtœ:r/

(iii) The exceptions to (ii), few if any of them in widespread use, include *veule* and *jeûne* (see 10.7.2), (*la vache*) *beugle* /bø:gl/, *émeute* /emø:t/, *feutre* /fø:tr/, (*la vache*) *meugle* /mø:gl/, *meule* /mø:l/, *meute* /mø:t/ and *neutre* /nø:tr/.

10.7.5   In open stressed syllables, the pronunciation is *always* /ø/, e.g. *deux* /dø/, *peu* /pø/, *bœufs* /bø/, *creux* /krø/, *nœud* /nø/, (*il*) *pleut* /plø/, (*il*) *veut* /vø/, *joyeux* /ʒwajø/.

10.7.6   In line with 10.7.4 and 10.7.5, note the difference in vowel between the singular forms *bœuf* /bœf/, *œuf* /œf/ and the corresponding plurals *bœufs* /bø/, *œufs* /ø/.

10.7.7   In unstressed syllables:

(i) The pronunciation is generally that of the corresponding stressed vowel where there is one, e.g.:

/ø/ *creuser* /krøze/, *joyeusement* /ʒwajøzmɑ̃/, *déjeuner* /deʒøne/ (from *jeûne*), *beugler* /bøgle/, *feutré* /føtre/, *neutron* /nøtrɔ̃/, *deuxième* /døzjɛm/, *pleuvoir* /pløvwa:r/

/œ/ *seulement* /sœlmɑ̃/, *meurtrier* /mœrtrije/, *neuvième* /nœvjɛm/, *feuillage* /fœja:ʒ/, *œillade* /œjad/, *ameublement* /amœbləmɑ̃/

(ii) Where there is no corresponding stressed syllable, the pronunciation is usually /ø/, e.g. *Europe* /ørɔp/, *euphémisme*

/øfemism/, *jeudi* /ʒødi/, *meunier* /mønje/, *neurologue* /nørɔlɔg/, *peuplier* /pøplije/ (no connection with *peuple*).

(iii) Despite what is said in (i) and (ii) above, it may be noted that there is considerable variation in usage and that, in many of the words quoted and others falling into the same category, either /ø/ or /œ/ or an intermediate vowel, i.e. an *eu moyen* (cf. 10.6.5), is acceptable. Among the more frequently occurring words, however, the pronunciations *deuxième* /døzjɛm/, *jeudi* /ʒødi/, *neuvième* /nœvjɛm/ and *seulement* /sœlmã/ should be adopted.

10.8 /o/ – High-Mid Back Rounded; /ɔ/ – Low-Mid Back Rounded

10.8.1 These two vowels, like /y/, /u/, /ø/ and /œ/, are pronounced with firmly rounded lips – much more so than the *o* of British English *not*, *dog*, etc. (which is itself more rounded than in most American pronunciations of the same words). However, the vowel of such words as *no*, *so* as pronounced by those northern English, Scottish and Welsh speakers who do not diphthongize their vowels approximates to French /o/ and the vowel of both British and American pronunciations of words such as *taught*, *lawn*, *call*, etc., is not far removed from (but considerably more relaxed than) that of French /ɔ/; the French vowel, however, is rather more open and somewhat further forward, and may be long or short, whereas the English vowel is always long.

10.8.2 As in the case of /e/ and /ɛ/ (10.6) and of /ø/ and /œ/ (10.7), our main problem is to define the conditions in which /o/ and /ɔ/ – or an intermediate vowel (see 10.8.8) – are used in stressed and unstressed syllables, closed or open.

10.8.3 In closed stressed syllables, either vowel may occur (note that, in these circumstances, /o/ is always long – see 12.5). The following guidelines cover nearly all cases:

(i) When the spelling is *ô*, *au* or *eau*, the pronunciation is /o/, e.g. *hôte* /oːt/, *côte* /koːt/, *diplôme* /diploːm/, *rôle* /roːl/, *paume* /poːm/, *hausse* /oːs/, *chaude* /ʃoːd/, *pauvre* /poːvr/, *heaume* /oːm/, (*la*) *Beauce* /boːs/ (but note the difference between the feminine and masculine first names *Paule* /poːl/, and *Paul* /pɔl/)

(ii) In *-ose*, the pronunciation is /o/, e.g. *rose* /roːz/, *chose* /ʃoːz/, (*il*) *ose* /oːz/

(iii) In *-ome*, *-one*, *-osse*, pronunciation varies from one word to another; the indications given in (iv)–(vi) cover most words in general use

(iv) *-ome* is pronounced /oːm/ in *arome* (also written *arôme*) /aroːm/, *home* /oːm/, *chrome* /kroːm/ and its derivatives *monochrome* and *polychrome*, and in *atome* /atoːm/, *axiome* /aksjoːm/ and *idiome* /idjoːm/ (do not be influenced by the pronunciation of English *atom*, *axiom*, *idiom*), but /ɔm/ in most other words in general use (and, in particular, in words in *-onome*), e.g. *tome* /tɔm/, *Rome* /rɔm/ (do not be influenced by the English pronunciation), *astronome* /astrɔnɔm/, *autonome* /ɔtɔnɔm/; note, however, that this rule does not cover a number of technical or infrequent terms (e.g. *rhizome* /-oːm/, *majordome* /-ɔm/), which should be looked up in a dictionary

(v) *-one* is pronounced /oːn/ in *cyclone* /sikloːn/ and *zone* /zoːn/ but /ɔn/ elsewhere, e.g. *carbone* /karbɔn/, *ozone* /ozɔn/, *téléphone* /telefɔn/

(vi) *-osse* is pronounced /oːs/ in the word *fosse* /foːs/, and in words related to *dos* /do/ and *gros* /gro/, principally (*il*) *s'adosse* /sadoːs/, (*il*) *endosse* /ãdoːs/, *grosse* /groːs/, but /ɔs/ in other words, e.g. *bosse* /bɔs/, *brosse* /brɔs/, *colosse* /kɔlɔs/, *Écosse* /ekɔs/

(vii) Elsewhere the pronunciation is /ɔ/ (long, i.e. /ɔː/, before /ʒ, r, v, vr/ – see 12.6), e.g. *somme* /sɔm/, *note* /nɔt/, *vote* /vɔt/, *forte* /fɔrt/, *nobl* /nɔbl/, *globe* /glɔb/, *mode* /mɔd/, *épisode* /epizɔd/, *école* /ekɔl/, *sole* /sɔl/, *poste* /pɔst/, *philosophe* /filɔzɔf/, (*il*) *vole* /vɔl/ (in many of these words, one must beware of being influenced by the corres-

ponding English word); note too that most words in -*um* have
the vowel /ɔ/, e.g. *rhum* /rɔm/, *chewing-gum* /ʃwiŋgɔm/,
album /albɔm/, *maximum* ≠maksimɔm/, *minimum*
/minimɔm/ (but *parfum* /parfœ̃/ is an exception); *loge* /lɔ:ʒ/,
horloge /ɔrlɔ:ʒ/, *Limoges* /limɔ:ʒ/, *mort* /mɔ:r/, (*il*) *adore*
/adɔ:r/, *sonore* /sɔnɔ:r/, (*il*) *innove* /inɔ:v/, *Hanovre*
/anɔ:vr/ (*Vosges* /vo:ʒ/ is an exception).

(viii) Note that, on the basis of (i), (iv) and (vii) above, it is
possible to have minimal pairs distinguished only by the
vowels /o:/ and /ɔ/, e.g.:

/o:/		/ɔ/	
côte	/ko:t/	cote	/kɔt/
paume	/po:m/	pomme	/pɔm/
heaume	/o:m/	homme	/ɔm/
hausse	/o:s/	os	/ɔs/
saule	/so:l/	sole	/sɔl/
rauque	/ro:k/	roc	/rɔk/

10.8.4 In open stressed syllables, there is no problem: the
pronunciation is *always* /o/, whatever the spelling, e.g. *beau*
/bo/, *chaud* /ʃo/, *dos* /do/, *gros* /gro/, *sabot* /sabo/, *loyaux*
/lwajo/.

10.8.5 In line with 10.8.3 and 10.8.4, note the difference in
vowel between the singular (*un*) *os* /ɔs/ 'bone' and the plural
(*des*) *os* /o/ 'bones'.

10.8.6 In closed unstressed syllables the pronunciation is
nearly always /ɔ/, e.g. *horloge* /ɔrlɔ:ʒ/, *hostile* /ɔstil/,
morceau /mɔrso/, *postal* /pɔstal/, *porter* /pɔrte/, *objet*
/ɔbʒɛ/, *oblique* /ɔblik/, *octave* /ɔkta:v/. The only significant
exceptions are a few derivatives of words having /o/ in a
stressed syllable, e.g. *fausseté* /foste/, *faussement* /fosmɑ̃/,
sauterie /sotri/, *gaucherie* /goʃri/, *gauchement* /goʃmɑ̃/,
sauvetage /sovta:ʒ/, corresponding to *faux*, (*il*) *saute*,

gauche, *sauf*, and future and conditional forms such as *j'oserai* /ʒozre/, (*il*) *posera* /pozra/, (*il*) *faucherait* /foʃrɛ/, etc., corresponding to (*il*) *ose, pose, fauche*, etc. In many other words, especially where the spelling is *au*, either /ɔ/ or /o/ is acceptable, e.g. *austère* /ɔstɛːr/ or /ostɛːr/, *augmenter* /ɔgmãte/ or /ogmãte/, *cauchemar* /kɔʃmaːr/ or /koʃmaːr/, *côtelette* /kɔtlɛt/ or /kotlɛt/.

10.8.7   In open unstressed syllables, the pronunciation is always /ɔ/ where there is a corresponding stressed syllable in /ɔ/, e.g. *écolier* /ekɔlje/, *global* /glɔbal/, *philosophique* /filɔzɔfik/, *pommier* /pɔmje/, *sonorité* /sɔnɔrite/, corresponding to *école, globe, philosophe, pomme, sonore*, and, in most cases, /o/ where there is a corresponding stressed vowel in /o/, e.g. *beaucoup* /boku/, *beauté* /bote/, *côté* /kote/, *grossier* /grosje/, *hauteur* /otœːr/, *jaunir* /ʒoniːr/, *rosier* /rozje/, *sauter* /sote/, corresponding to *beau* /bo/, *côte* /koːt/, *gros* /gro/, *haut* /o/, *jaune* /ʒoːn/, *rose* /roːz/, (*il*) *saute* /soːt/ (but note, as exceptions, *atomique* /atɔmik/, *idiomatique* /idjɔmatik/, *polaire* /pɔlɛːr/, beside *atome* /atoːm/, *idiome* /idjoːm/, *pôle* /poːl/).

Elsewhere, the pronunciation is /ɔ/ in most words, e.g. *diplomate* /diplɔmat/, *forêt* /fɔrɛ/, *fromage* /frɔmaːʒ/, *honnête* /ɔnɛt/, *horizon* /ɔrizõ/, *joli* /ʒɔli/, *moment* /mɔmã/, *moteur* /mɔtœːr/, *olive* /ɔliːv/, *oreille* /ɔrɛj/, *potage* /pɔtaːʒ/, *programme* /prɔgram/, *total* /tɔtal/, *volet* /vɔlɛ/. Note that this also applies to the prefix *co-* in hiatus with a following vowel, e.g. *coexister* /kɔɛgziste/, *cohabitation* /kɔabitasjõ/, *cohérent* /kɔerã/, *coopérer* /kɔɔpere/, *coordonner* /kɔɔrdone/.

/o/ occurs however in the following circumstances:

(i) in many words having the spelling *au*, e.g. *aubergine* /obɛrʒin/, *aucun* /okœ̃/, *aussi* /osi/, *autant* /otã/, *auteur* /otœːr/, *chauffeur* /ʃofœːr/, *chausser* /ʃose/, *dauphin* /dofɛ̃/, *fauteuil* /fotœj/

(ii) before /z/, e.g. *arroser* /aroze/, *groseille* /grozɛj/, *position* /pozisjõ/, *roseau* /rozo/

(iii) in the ending -*otion*, e.g. *dévotion* /devosjɔ̃/, *émotion* /emosjɔ̃/, *promotion* /prɔmosjɔ̃/, *notion* /nosjɔ̃/.

In many words, either pronunciation is possible, e.g. *autel* /ɔtɛl/ or /otɛl/, *auto* /ɔto/ or /oto/, *automne* /ɔtɔn/ or /otɔn/, *fossile* /fɔsil/ or /fosil/, *hôpital* /ɔpital/ (the more usual pronunciation) or /opital/, *hôtel* /ɔtɛl/ or /otɛl/, *mauvais* /mɔvɛ/ or /movɛ/, *naufrage* /nɔfraːʒ/ or /nofraːʒ/, *rôtir* /rɔtiːr/ or /rotiːr/; note that this also applies to the future and conditional of the verbs *avoir*, *falloir*, *savoir* and *valoir*, e.g. *nous aurons* /ɔrɔ̃/ or /orɔ̃/, (*il*) *faudra* /fɔdra/ or /fodra/, (*je*) *saurai* /sɔre/ or /sore/, (*il*) *vaudrait* /vɔdrɛ/ or /vodrɛ/.

10.8.8 Alternatively, as in the case of /e/ and /ɛ/ (10.6.5 (i)) and of /ø/ and /œ/ (10.7.7 (iii)), an intermediate vowel, i.e. a vowel somewhere between /o/ and /ɔ/, is often heard in unstressed syllables, either closed or open.

10.9 /a/ – Low Front Unrounded; /ɑ/ – Low Back Rounded

10.9.1 It must be stressed at the outset that, in a sense, there is no problem since many native speakers of French no longer distinguish between these two vowels, using /a/ instead of /ɑ/ in all circumstances. Many speakers, particularly non-Parisians, still do use /ɑ/, particularly in stressed position and particularly in the case of a few words such as *pas* /pɑ/ and *trois* /trwɑ/ and before /z/, e.g. *base* /bɑːz/, *emphase* /ɑ̃fɑːz/, *phrase* /frɑːz/, but the foreign learner who prefers to make life simpler by pronouncing /a/ even in such words as these is in good company and is unlikely to attract criticism. The indications that follow are, therefore, descriptive of only one, and that a rather conservative, type of pronunciation and may, if the reader wishes, be ignored. On the other hand, in some varieties of what is considered as a sub-standard Parisian pronunciation, the difference between the two vowels is exaggerated, with the result that the vowel of *pas* approaches that of English *paw*. This pronunciation should not be copied.

10.9.2   The front vowel /a/ is very similar to that of the vowel of words such as *cat*, *man*, pronounced with a Welsh or a Yorkshire accent – the vowel of the same words in RP (see 1.1.3) is higher (between /a/ and /ɛ/ – the symbol for it is /æ/) and is *not* an adequate substitute for the French vowel.

10.9.3   The pronunciation of the back vowel /ɑ/ is not dissimilar to the RP pronunciation of the *a* of *glass*, *past*, etc. (but it is very different from the Welsh or Yorkshire pronunciation of such words, which has the same vowel as in *cat*, *man*, etc., and from the North American pronunciation of such words which has a higher and front vowel). The French vowel, however, is more rounded and, depending on its phonetic context, may be either long or short (see 12.3 to 12.5).

10.9.4   In stressed syllables, although it is now acceptable to pronounce the vowel as /a/ (see 10.9.1), the pronunciation of /ɑ/ is still widespread or even usual in a number of words. The following are among the most common of these:
   (i) (with the spelling *a*, i.e. without an accent) *bas*, *basse* /bɑ, bɑːs/, *base* /bɑːz/, *cadre* /kɑːdr/, *cas* /kɑ/, *classe* /klɑːs/, *diable* /djɑːbl/, *fable* /fɑːbl/, *flamme* /flɑːm/, *gars* /gɑ/, *gaz* /gɑːz/, *gras*, *grasse* /grɑ, grɑːs/, *hélas* /helɑːs/, *miracle* /mirɑːkl/, *paille* /pɑːj/, *pas* /pɑ/, (*je*) *passe* /pɑːs/, *phase* /fɑːz/, *phrase* /frɑːz/, *rail* /rɑːj/, *rare* /rɑːr/, (*je*) *rase* /rɑːz/, *repas* /rəpɑ/, *sable* /sɑːbl/, *tas* /tɑ/, *tasse* /tɑːs/, *vase* /vɑːz/
   (ii) (with the spelling *â*) *âge* /ɑːʒ/, *âme* /ɑːm/, *âpre* /ɑːpr/, *blâme* /blɑːm/, *câble* /kɑːbl/, *crâne* /krɑːn/, (*je*) *gâte* /gɑːt/, *grâce* /grɑːs/, *hâte* /ɑːt/, *mâle* /mɑːl/, *pâle* /pɑːl/, *Pâques* /pɑːk/, *pâte* /pɑːt/, *plâtre* /plɑːtr/, *tâche* /tɑːʃ/
   (iii) (with the spelling *oi*, especially after /r/) (*le*) *bois*

/bwɑ/, (je) crois, (il) croit /krwɑ/, croix /krwɑ/, droit /drwɑ/, endroit /ɑ̃drwɑ/, étroit /etrwɑ/, froid /frwɑ/, roi /rwɑ/, voix /vwɑ/.

10.9.5 Among words in -as, -asse, -able that normally or invariably take /a/, note bras /bra/, chasse /ʃas/, (que je, qu'il) fasse /fas/, masse /mas/, table /tabl/ and adjectives in -able such as capable /kapabl/ and raisonnable /rɛzɔnabl/.

10.9.6 In so far as the distinction between /a/ and /ɑ/ is observed, we have minimal pairs such as the following (note that stressed /ɑ/ in a closed syllable is always long – see 12.5):

/a/	/ɑ/
(il) bat /ba/,	bas /bɑ/
(je) bois, (il) boit /bwa/	(le) bois /bwɑ/
là /la/	las /lɑ/
(je) vois, (il) voit, (la) voie /vwa/	(la) voix /vwɑ/
mal, malle /mal/	mâle /mɑːl/
patte /pat/	pâte /pɑːt/
tache /taʃ/	tâche /tɑːʃ/

10.9.7 In unstressed syllables, the pronunciation /ɑ/ is appreciably less common than in stressed syllables. Among words in which it is still relatively current (most of them having corresponding words with a stressed syllable in /ɑ/) are âprement /aprəmɑ̃/, âpreté /aprəte/, bâtir /bɑtiːr/, bâton /bɑtɔ̃/, blâmer /blame/, gâteau /gɑto/, gâter /gɑte/, navrant /navrɑ̃/, pâlir /pɑliːr/, pâté /pate/, raser /rɑze/, tâcher /taʃe/.

Note that many words are generally or invariably pronounced with /a/ even where there is a corresponding stressed syllable having /ɑ/, e.g. boisé /bwaze/, classique /klasik/, enflammé /ɑ̃flame/, paillasse /pajas/, passage /pasaːʒ/, royal /rwajal/.

Both pronunciations occur in words in -ation, e.g. nation /nasjɔ̃/ or /nɑsjɔ̃/, occupation /ɔkypasjɔ̃/ or /ɔkypɑsjɔ̃/, *civilisation* /sivilizasjɔ̃/ or /sivilizɑsjɔ̃/, and in *passion* /pasjɔ̃/ or /pɑsjɔ̃/, but the pronunciation in /a/ is the more usual.

10.10   The Nasal Vowels

10.10.1   It is sometimes argued that the term 'nasal vowel' is inappropriate since, when the vowels in question are being uttered, the air escapes through the mouth as well as through the nose, and that the term 'naso-oral' is therefore more accurate. This is true, but the term 'nasal' has long been in general use and there is no good reason not to continue to use it.

The tongue and lip positions of the nasal vowels /ɛ̃/, /œ̃/, /ɔ̃/ and /ɑ̃/ are, as we shall see in 10.10.2 to 10.10.5, only approximately the same as those for the corresponding oral vowels /ɛ/, /œ/, /ɔ/, /ɑ/.

It is essential to bear in mind – and, if necessary, to make a conscious effort to observe – the fact that, at the end of a group (as in *c'est bien* /sɛ bjɛ̃/ or *il est bon* /il ɛ bɔ̃/), or before a consonant (as in *sainte* /sɛ̃:t/, *humble* /œ̃:bl/, *tomber* /tɔ̃be/, *lentement* /lɑ̃tmɑ̃/, *une grande rue* /yn grɑ̃d ry/), there is *no nasal consonant* following the nasal vowel. There is a widespread tendency among English-speaking (and other foreign) learners of French to pronounce an [ŋ] (= the English *ng*) in words like *bon*, *grand*, an [n] in words like *sainte*, *ronde*, *monter*, *grandeur*, or an [m] in words like *grimper*, *humble*, *tomber*, *embarras*, *ample*. This must be avoided: the written nasal consonant, *n* or *m*, merely indicates that the preceding vowel is nasalized. (It is true that very many southern speakers of French either use a fleeting [ŋ]-type consonant after a nasal vowel, e.g. *grand* [grɑ̃ŋ], or even fail to nasalize the vowel at all before a consonant and so pronounce *demander*, *tomber*, etc., as [dəmande], [tɔmbe], etc. This is all very well if one is speaking consistently with an authentic southern accent – but for a foreigner who is basically trying to speak Parisian French to do so is a different matter altogether.)

The *only* circumstances in which a nasal vowel can be followed immediately by a nasal consonant are:

(i) in a small number of liaison forms such as *en été* /ɑ̃n ete/, *bien aimable* /bjɛ̃n ɛmabl/, *mon ami* /mɔ̃n ami/ (see 19.3.6)

(ii) in a very limited number of words (and their derivatives) beginning with *emm-* or *en-*, principally the following: *emmagasiner* /ɑ̃magazine/, *emmailloter* /ɑ̃majɔte/, *emmancher* /ɑ̃mɑ̃ʃe/, *emmêler* /ɑ̃mele/, *emmener* /ɑ̃mne/, *emmerder* /ɑ̃mɛrde/, *emmitoufler* /ɑ̃mitufle/, *emmurer* /ɑ̃myre/, *enamouré* /ɑ̃namure/, *enivrer* /ɑ̃nivre/, *enneigé* /ɑ̃neʒe/, *ennoblir* /ɑ̃nɔbliːr/, *ennuagé* /ɑ̃nɥaʒe/, *ennui* /ɑ̃nɥi/.

(iii) in the words *immangeable* /ɛ̃mɑ̃ʒabl/, and *immanquable* /ɛ̃mɑ̃kabl/.

10.10.2 /ɛ̃/ – low-mid front unrounded

The vowel /ɛ̃/ is a more open vowel than its oral equivalent /ɛ/ – its degree of aperture corresponds more to that of English /æ/ as in the RP pronunciation of *cat*.

/ɛ̃/ is represented in spelling primarily by *in*, *im*, e.g. *vin* /vɛ̃/, *important* /ɛ̃pɔrtɑ̃/, by *ain*, *aim*, e.g. *pain* /pɛ̃/, *faim* /fɛ̃/, by *ein*, e.g. *plein* /plɛ̃/, or (especially in the groups *ien*, *yen*) by *en*, e.g. *bien* /bjɛ̃/, *(il) tient* /tjɛ̃/, *moyen* /mwajɛ̃/, *appendicite* /apɛ̃disit/, *examen* /ɛgzamɛ̃/. The spellings *ym*, *yn* occur in a few words, especially in the prefixes *sym-*, *syn-*, before a consonant, e.g. *symbole* /sɛ̃bɔl/, *sympathique* /sɛ̃patik/, *symphonie* /sɛ̃fɔni/, *symptôme* /sɛ̃ptoːm/, *syndicat* /sɛ̃dika/, *syntaxe* /sɛ̃tax/, and in *thym* /tɛ̃/.

/ɛ̃/ is also very frequently substituted for /œ̃/ (see 10.10.3).

10.10.3 /œ̃/ – low-mid front rounded

Just as /ɛ̃/ is a more open vowel than /ɛ/, likewise /œ̃/ is more open than /œ/. It is usually represented by the spelling *un*, e.g. *un* /œ̃/, *brun* /brœ̃/, *lundi* /lœ̃di/, *emprunter* /ɑ̃prœ̃te/; apart from a few place-names, the only contexts in which it is represented by anything other than *un* are *humble* /œ̃:bl/, *parfum* /parfœ̃/, and *à jeûn* /a ʒœ̃/.

It should be noted that there is a widespread tendency in Parisian pronunciation, including the careful speech of highly educated Parisians, to substitute /ɛ̃/ for /œ̃/, e.g. *un* /ɛ̃/, *aucun* /okɛ̃/, *brun* /brɛ̃/, *chacun* /ʃakɛ̃/, *commun* /kɔmɛ̃/, *Dunkerque* /dɛ̃kɛrk/, *emprunter* /ɑ̃prɛ̃te/, *humble* /ɛ̃:bl/, *lundi* /lɛ̃di/, *opportun* /ɔpɔrtɛ̃/, *quelqu'un* /kɛlkɛ̃/. This feature is now so well established that there is no reason why foreigners should not adopt it. It should be noted however that the pronunciation /œ̃/ still remains in certain parts of France and, indeed, in the speech of many Parisians, particularly those of the older generation.

10.10.4 /ɔ̃/ – mid back rounded

Whereas, as we have seen (10.10.2 and 10.10.3), the nasal vowels /ɛ̃/ and /œ̃/ are more open than their oral equivalents /ɛ/ and /œ/, the vowel /ɔ̃/ is *less* open than /ɔ/. In terms of its degree of aperture and of lip-rounding, it comes between /ɔ/ and /o/ and is, indeed, somewhat closer to /o/ than to /ɔ/. For this reason, many books on French pronunciation represent it by the symbol /õ/. The only valid reason for continuing to use /ɔ̃/, as is the case in this book, is that that is the standard IPA transcription and that it is used in the main French–English dictionaries.

With the exception of a few technical terms, some of them very rare, e.g. *lumbago* /lɔ̃bago/, *unguifère* /ɔ̃gɥifɛ:r/), and a small number of foreign words such as *jungle* /ʒɔ̃:gl/, *tungsten* /tɔ̃gstɛn/ (also – and more usually – pronounced /ʒœ̃:gl/, /tœ̃gstɛn/), the spelling is always *on*, e.g. *bon* /bɔ̃/, *long* /lɔ̃/, *monter* /mɔ̃te/, or *om*, e.g. *ombre* /ɔ̃:br/, *tomber* /tɔ̃be/.

On the need to distinguish clearly between /ɔ̃/ and /ɑ̃/, see 10.10.6.

10.10.5 /ɑ̃/ – low back rounded

/ɑ̃/ is rather less open than its oral equivalent, /ɑ/. Note however that, whereas /ɑ/ is often replaced by /a/ (see

10.9.1), /ã/ is always pronounced as a back vowel. Apart from a few proper names (e.g. *Laon* /lã/, *Saint-Saëns* /sɛ̃sã:s/), the spelling is always *an*, *am*, *en* or *em*, e.g. *chanter* /ʃãte/, *dans* /dã/, *sang* /sã/, *champignon* /ʃãpiɲɔ̃/, *lampe* /lã:p/, *cent* /sã/, *menton* /mãtɔ̃/, *temps* /tã/.

10.10.6 It is very noticeable that many foreigners fail to make the distinction between /ã/ and /ɔ̃/. The two vowels must however be clearly distinguished. Those who detect a failure in their own pronunciation to differentiate between members of such pairs as the following should, therefore, make a conscious effort to do so:

/ɔ̃/		/ã/	
blond	/blɔ̃/	*blanc*	/blã/
don, *dont*	/dɔ̃/	*dans*, *dent*	/dã/
long	/lɔ̃/	*lent*	/lã/
(*nous*) *montons*	/mɔ̃tɔ̃/	(*nous*) *mentons*	/mãtɔ̃/
ronger	/rɔ̃ʒe/	*ranger*	/rãʒe/
son, *sont*	/sɔ̃/	*cent*, *sang*, *sans*	/sã/
ton, *thon*	/tɔ̃/	*tant*, *temps*	/tã/
tromper	/trɔ̃pe/	*tremper*	/trãpe/

10.11 Unvoicing of Vowels

Whereas in many other languages vowels are normally fully voiced throughout, one result of the tenseness of French articulation is that the last fraction of a vowel before a pause is not infrequently voiceless – i.e. the vocal cords stop vibrating while the lip- and tongue-positions for the vowel are maintained and air continues to be expelled from the lungs. If we indicate this unvoiced segment by a superscript form of the appropriate vowel symbol and the symbol for voicelessness [˳] (see 18.2.2), we can represent the pronunciation of vowels in these circumstances as follows:

oui [wi^{i}], *je l'ai vu* [ʒə le vy^{y}], *c'est tout* [sɛ tu^{u}]

(Note that this form of transcription does *not* indicate any lengthening of the vowel.) This phenomenon is particularly common, as in the above examples, with the three high vowels, /i/, /y/ and /u/, but may also occur elsewhere, especially with the high-mid vowels /e/, /ø/ and /o/, e.g.:

> *vive la liberté* [viv la libɛrteᵉ], *je le veux* [ʒə l vøᵒ], *qu'il est beau* [kil ɛ boᵒ].

We draw attention to this feature for recognition purposes only. There is no need for foreign learners to make a determined effort to adopt it, but they should be aware of its existence.

10.12   Canadianisms

10.12.1   There is, of course, considerable variation in pronunciation within the province of Quebec, both regionally and individually, ranging from those whose pronunciation is virtually indistinguishable from that of Parisians to those whose Quebec accent is so strong as to be difficult to understand for those whose ear is accustomed only to European French. Only three of the more widespread and striking features of the pronunciation of vowels are mentioned here for recognition purposes; of these, those noted in 10.12.2 and 10.12.3 are more likely to occur in educated speech than that noted in 10.12.4. (For a full discussion of Canadian French vowels, see Walker, 1984: chapter 3.)

10.12.2   There is a widespread tendency to give short /i/, /y/ and /u/ a more open pronunciation than in European French. These varieties can be represented as [ɪ], [ʏ] and [ʊ]; [ɪ] and [ʊ] are pronounced rather like the vowels of English *bit* and *put* respectively but, of course, with greater tension; e.g.:

facile	[fasɪl]	*jupe*	[ʒʏp]	*bouche*	[buʃ]
liquide	[lɪkɪd]	*musique*	[mʏzik]	*cousine*	[kʊzɪn]
riche	[rɪʃ]	*plume*	[plʏm]	*soupe*	[sʊp]
vite	[vɪt]	*tu l'as vu?*	[tʏ la vʏ]	*toute*	[tʊt]

10.12.3 The vowel /ɑ̃/ as in *attends!*, *je suis content*, *le temps*, may have a less open pronunciation than in standard French and, to an ear that is not accustomed to it, can sound more like the /ɛ̃/ of *vin*, *pain*, etc.

10.12.4 Some Quebec speakers diphthongize long vowels in certain circumstances. This is particularly noticeable in the case of /ɛ:/ and /ɑ:/, which are liable to become [ɛj] or [aj] and [ɑw] respectively, e.g. *frère* [frɛjr] or [frajr], *prêtre* [prɛjtr̥] or [prajtr̥], *phrase* [frɑwz], *câble* [kɑwbl̥].

11 Mute e

11.1 Introduction

11.1.1 The vowel known as mute *e* (for other terms applied to it, see 4.9.1) is a front vowel pronounced in much the same part of the mouth as the vowels /ø/ and /œ/. It is often considered to be an unstressed allophone of one or other of these (if anything, it is closer to /œ/ than to /ø/). Indeed, a survey made in 1971 (Dauzes, 1973: 36) showed that many Parisian teenagers and some adults failed to distinguish between such pairs as *ample rang* /ɑ̃plə rɑ̃/ and *en pleurant* /ɑ̃ plœrɑ̃/, *elle se le demande* /ɛl sə l dəmɑ̃ːd/ and *elle seule demande* /ɛl sœl dəmɑ̃ːd/, *c'est comme je dis* /sɛ kɔm ʒə di/ and *c'est comme jeudi* /sɛ kɔm ʒødi/, using an *eu moyen* (see 10.7.7 (iii)) in all cases. Another survey, published in 1977, of the way people actually speak (as distinct from the way normative works say they *ought* to speak) also concluded that the way in which the vowel in question is pronounced varies from one speaker to another but that, particularly in Paris, most pronounce it 'exactement de la même manière que l'un des phonèmes de la série antérieure /ø/ ou /œ/' (Walter, 1977: 50).

However, the fact remains that /ə/, however it may be pronounced when it *is* pronounced, can often be omitted altogether (which is largely what this chapter is about), while /ø/ and /œ/ as traditionally defined are never omitted, even when unstressed. This seems to provide sufficient justification, at the purely practical level, for treating /ə/ separately.

11.1.2 Two points need to be borne in mind:

(i) /ə/ is a *rounded* vowel – it is not the same as the vowel of unstressed English *the* or the second syllable of *clever* or of *liberate*, a vowel that is usually represented in phonetic transcriptions of English by the same symbol, /ə/; the French vowel is pronounced rather further forward in the mouth and with noticeably rounded lips

(ii) it cannot be stressed; in contexts in which the pronoun *le* follows an imperative verb and is stressed, it is pronounced /lø/, e.g. *dites-le!* /dit lø/, *prenez-le!* /prəne lø/; likewise in the expression *sur ce* /syr sø/ 'thereupon'.

11.1.3 It is always written *e*, except in the first syllable of *faisan* /fəzã/ and of related words, in *monsieur* /məsjø/, and in some parts of the verb *faire*, namely *faisant* /fəzã/, (*nous*) *faisons* /fəzɔ̃/ and throughout the imperfect indicative tense, (*je*) *faisais* /fəzɛ/, etc.

11.1.4 The main problem with mute *e* is to know when to pronounce it and when not. To take two simple examples of very frequent types of situation:

(i) the *e* of the first syllable of *fenêtre* is pronounced in *une fenêtre* /yn fənɛtr/ but not (or not normally) in *la fenêtre* /la fnɛtr/

(ii) *car je le ferai* is pronounced /kar ʒə l fəre/ (i.e. the mute *e* is pronounced in *je* and *ferai* but not in *le*) whereas *et je le ferai* is pronounced /e ʒ lə fre/ (i.e., this time the mute *e* is pronounced in *le* but not in *je* or *ferai*) (see Fouché, 1969: 106–7).

The full picture is in fact extremely complicated – Fouché, for example, devotes nearly fifty pages to it (1969: 91–139) (and used to tell foreign students following his course in French phonetics at the Sorbonne that no foreigner would ever succeed in fully mastering the complexities of the matter: he was probably right).

That, however, is not a counsel of despair. By way of encouragement to the foreign learner, it can be said that a great deal can be done by way of simplification. In particular, we shall give:

(i) just four very simple 'rules' that will cover the majority of cases (see 11.2) but which, because they take no account of a number of exceptions, represent the extreme of simplification

(ii) an expanded version of these four rules that will cover the great majority of cases (see 11.3).

11.2   Four Simple 'Rules'

11.2.1   Here, as in dealing with other aspects of French pronunciation, it must be remembered that the relevant phonetic unit is not the word but the group (see chapter 7).

If the following 'rules' are observed, the pronunciation adopted in respect of mute *e* will be correct in a substantial majority of cases. Where the fact of observing the rules leads the foreigner to pronounce an /ə/ where a native-speaker would not normally do so, the result will not be such as to shock the native-speaker and the learner is therefore advised, in cases of doubt, to pronounce rather than omit the /ə/.

11.2.2   **Rule 1:**   at the end of a group, /ə/ is not pronounced in Parisian French (on regional French, see 11.4), e.g. *la porte* /la pɔrt/, *trop vaste* /tro vast/, *les Alpes* /lez alp/, *sur l'arbre* /syr larbr/, *sous la table* /su la tabl/, *je vais le vendre* /ʒə vɛ l vɑ̃:dr/, *à la fin du siècle* /a la fɛ̃ dy sjɛkl/ (see also 11.10 and 16.5.3).

11.2.3   **Rule 2:**   in the first syllable of a group, /ə/ is normally pronounced (for exceptions, see 11.5.2), e.g. *de quelle manière?* /də kɛl manjɛ:r/, *je sais* /ʒə sɛ/, *le beau livre* /lə bo li:vr/, *le voulez-vous?* /lə vule vu/, *me comprends-tu?*

/mə kɔ̃prɑ̃ ty/, *ne dites pas ça* /nə dit pɑ sa/, *demain matin*
/dəmɛ̃ matɛ̃/, *levez-vous* /ləve vu/, *selon moi* /səlɔ̃ mwa/,
tenacement /tənasmɑ̃/.

11.2.4 Rule 3:   within a group (i.e. when it is neither in the
first syllable nor at the end), mute *e* is generally *not* pronounced if it is preceded by only one consonant (i.e. of course
one *pronounced* consonant) (for exceptions, see 11.6); to
make the point clear, the unpronounced vowel in question is
enclosed in parentheses in the examples that follow: *mais j(e)*
veux l(e) faire /mɛ ʒ vø l fɛːr/, *ne m(e) comprends-tu pas?*
/nə m kɔ̃prɑ̃ ty pɑ/, *tu vas t(e) faire mal* /ty va t fɛr mal/, *vous*
l(e) verrez /vu l vɛre/, *il va s(e) contenter d(e) ça* /il va s
kɔ̃tɑ̃te d sa/, *vous voyez l(e) problème* /vu vwaje l prɔblɛm/,
vous n(e) comprenez pas /vu n kɔ̃prəne pɑ/, *un kilo d(e)*
pommes /œ̃ kilo d pɔm/, *pas d(e) problème* /pɑ d prɔblɛm/,
vous prenez c(e) vin? /vu prəne s vɛ̃/, *tu sais qu(e) c'est faux*
/ty sɛ k sɛ fo/, *ouvrez la f(e)nêtre* /uvre la fnɛtr/, *j'ai r(e)çu ta*
lettre /ʒe rsy ta lɛtr/, *il n'est pas v(e)nu* /il nɛ pɑ vny/, *vous*
v(e)nez? /vu vne/, *à d(e)main* /a dmɛ̃/, *(je) chant(e)rai*
/ʃɑ̃tre/, *je vais l'app(e)ler* /ʒə vɛ l aple/, *(la) bouch(e)rie*
/buʃri/, *(le) jug(e)ment* /ʒyʒmɑ̃/, *(des) renseign(e)ments*
/rɑ̃sɛɲmɑ̃/, *all(e)mand* /almɑ̃/, *dang(e)reux* /dɑ̃ʒrø/,
lent(e)ment /lɑ̃tmɑ̃/, *sam(e)di* /samdi/.

In contexts in which the operation of this 'rule' brings
together two identical consonants, e.g. *je l(e) lave* /ʒə l laːv/,
là-d(e)dans /laddɑ̃/, *honnêt(e)té* /ɔnɛtte/, see chapter 17.

11.2.5 Rule 4:   within a group, mute *e* generally *is* pronounced if it is preceded by two or more pronounced
consonants (for exceptions, see 11.7); the consonants and
vowel in question are printed in bold type in the following
examples: *car je l(e) dirai* /kar ʒə l dire/, *il me fait peur* /il mə
fɛ pœːr/, *il te verra* /il tə vɛra/, *pour le dire* /pur lə diːr/, *un*
quar(t) de rouge /œ̃ kar də ruːʒ/, *Paul ne veut pas* /pɔl nə vø
pɑ/, *(le)* gouve**r**nement /guvɛrnəmɑ̃/, *(la)* **me**rcerie
/mɛrsəri/, *(le)* **pa**rlement /parləmɑ̃/, *(le)* po**rte**feuille

/pɔrtəfœj/, (la) propreté /prɔprəte/, le premier /lə prəmje/, vendredi /vãdrədi/, fortement /fɔrtəmã/, horriblement /ɔribləmã/, justement /ʒystəmã/, par-dessus /pardəsy/, pour demain /pur dəmɛ̃/, il a crevé /il a krəve/, il parle trop /il parlə tro/, la porte principale /la pɔrtə prɛ̃sipal/.

In the following examples, the fact that one mute e is not pronounced, in accordance with rule 3, means that two consonants are brought together and that, consequently a second mute e is pronounced in accordance with rule 4: et j(e) le dirai /e ʒ lə dire/, tu l(e) demandes /ty l dəmã:d/, vous l(e) ferez /vu le fəre/, Henri n(e) me connaît pas /ãri n mə kɔnɛ pɑ/, un(e) fenêtre /yn fənɛtr/, la grand(e) fenêtre /la grãd fənɛtr/, Pierr(e) le dit /pjɛr lə di/.

11.3   An Expansion of the Four 'Rules'

As was made clear in 11.1 above, three of the four 'rules' given in 11.2 (i.e. all except rule 1) are highly simplified. If followed in conjunction with the advice given in 11.2.1 to pronounce the /ə/ in case of doubt, they will lead to what might be termed 'minimally acceptable' practice. Most learners however will want a more subtle analysis of normal French practice, and that we aim to provide in sections 11.4–11.7, where each of the rules is restated in an expanded and, in some respects, modified form. In particular, we shall pay attention where necessary to:

 (i) conditions in which the rule *must* be applied
 (ii) *some* of the more frequently recurring circumstances in which the rule is likely not to be applied in conversational usage, although it is also acceptable to do so
(iii) exceptions to the rule.

It must, however, be stressed again (see 11.1) that the whole question of the circumstances in which mute e is or is not pronounced, or is optionally pronounced, is a particularly complicated one and that even the expanded version of the 'rules' given below in fact represents a substantial simplification. The reader who wants to go into the topic in greater detail is referred to the very full treatment of it by Fouché (1969: 91–139).

11.4 Rule 1

Rule 1: at the end of a group, /ə/ is not pronounced in Parisian French.

There are no exceptions to this in Parisian French, but in much of the south of France /ə/ is regularly pronounced in all positions, including at the end of a group. Consequently, in the areas in question one may hear such pronunciations as *tu vas le perdre* /ty va lə pɛrdrə/, *une petite fillette* /ynə pətitə fijɛtə/.

11.5 Rule 2

Rule 2: in the first syllable of a group, /ə/ is normally pronounced.

11.5.1 The rule *must* be applied in the following circumstances:

(i) when the mute *e* is preceded by two consonants, e.g. *Bretons et Basques* /brətɔ̃ e bask/, *crevant* /krəvɑ̃/, *première-ment* /prəmjɛrmɑ̃/, *prenez-les!* /prəne le/, and the place-names *Grenade* /grənad/, *Stenay* /stənɛ/.

(ii) where two identical stops would otherwise come together, e.g. *que cachez-vous?* /kə kaʃe vu/, *te trouve-t-elle beau?* /tə truv t ɛl bo/ (this does not necessarily apply to other consonants but, in general, the learner is advised to pronounce the /ə/ in such contexts, e.g. *je joue* /ʒə ʒu/, *le lit* /lə li/, *me mens-tu?* /mə mɑ̃ ty/)

(iii) in *je ne*, e.g. *je ne veux pas* /ʒə n vø pɑ/

(iv) before certain combinations of consonant + semi-consonant, e.g. *ce lion* /sə ljɔ̃/, *le roi* /lə rwa/, including in

particular the frequently occurring contexts *je suis* /ʒə sɥi/
and *je lui* + verb, e.g. *je lui donne dix francs* /ʒə lɥi dɔn di frɑ̃/,
and the first and second persons plural of the conditional
tense of *être* and *faire*, viz. *serions, seriez, ferions, feriez*, e.g.
serions-nous admis? /sərjɔ̃ nu admi/, *feriez-vous cela?* /fərje
vu sla/

   (v) when the second syllable also contains a mute *e*, e.g. *ce
chemin* /sə ʃmɛ/, *le genou* /lə ʒnu/, *le fera-t-il?* /lə fra t il/,
me regardiez-vous? /mə rgardje vu/, *ne sera-t-il pas là?* /nə
sra t il pɑ la/, *ne me dites pas ça!* /nə m dit pɑ sa/, *que tenez-
vous?* /kə tne vu/, *que je vous plains!* /kə ʒ vu plɛ̃/, *que le
soleil est beau!* /kə l sɔlɛj ɛ bo/, *que se disent-ils?* /kə s dizt il/,
revenez demain /rəvne dmɛ̃/, *recevait-il ce journal?* /rəsvɛt il
sə ʒurnal/; however, this does not necessarily apply to *ce, se*
or *je* followed by a stop (see 11.5.2 (i)) or to *je me* and *je le*
which are frequently pronounced /ʒmə/, /ʒlə/, e.g. *je me
demande* /ʒ mə dmɑ̃:d/, *je le connais* /ʒ lə kɔnɛ/.

11.5.2 /ə/ is frequently dropped in such circumstances as
the following:
   (i) between /s/ or /ʒ/ (particularly in *ce, je*) and a stop, e.g.
ce que vous dites /s kə vu dit/ (*ce que* is nearly always
pronounced /skə/ in conversation), *ce qui me plaît* /s ki m
plɛ/, *ce petit chien* /s pəti ʃjɛ̃/, *cependant* /spɑ̃dɑ̃/, *se peut-il
que (...)?* /s pø t il kə/, *se connaissent-ils?* /s kɔnɛs t il/, *se
tenait-il bien?* /s tənɛt il bjɛ̃/, *je pars maintenant* /ʒ par
mɛ̃tnɑ̃/, *je demande à vous voir* /ʒ dəmɑ̃d a vu vwa:r/, *je te dis
une chose* /ʒ tə di yn ʃo:z/
   (ii) (less frequently than in the circumstances referred to in
(i) above) between /s/ or /ʒ/ and a consonant other than a
stop, e.g. *ce n'est pas beau* /s nɛ pɑ bo/, *ce matin* /s matɛ̃/,
cela me plaît /sla m plɛ/, *se lave-t-il?* /s lav t il/, *je vais le faire*
/ʒ vɛ l fɛ:r/, *je vous crois* /ʒ vu krwɑ/, *je n'en veux pas* /ʒ nɑ̃ vø
pɑ/ (but see 11.5.1 (v) above)
   (iii) not infrequently in other circumstances, e.g. *demain
matin* /dmɛ̃ matɛ̃/, *venez me voir* /vne m vwa:r/, *petit idiot!*
/ptit idjo/, *que voulez-vouz?* /k vule vu/ – but only such

forms as have actually been heard in conversation should be used by foreigners, particularly those who tend to speak rather slowly (in which case the dropping of /ə/ is in any event less frequent than in rapid speech).

11.6   Rule 3

Rule 3: within a group, mute *e* is not pronounced if it is preceded by only one consonant.

11.6.1   As this rule is stated negatively (/ə/ is *not* pronounced), in this paragraph we shall begin with the exceptions to the rule. In that way, the expanded version of all three of these rules will begin with the cases when /ə/ is pronounced and end with those where it is not.

11.6.2   The main exceptions to the rule, i.e. the cases where /ə/ must be pronounced, are the following:

(i) when it is followed by /lj/, /nj/ or /rj/, e.g. *vous appeliez* /vuz apəlje/ (contrast *vous appelez* /vuz aple/), *atelier* /atəlje/, *hôtelier* /ɔtəlje/, *il n'y a pas de lions* /il ni a pɑ də ljɔ̃/ (alternatively, /il ni a pɑ d liɔ̃/), *Montpellier* /mɔ̃pəlje/, *Richelieu* /riʃəljø/, *nous venions* /nu vənjɔ̃/ (contrast *nous venons* /nu vnɔ̃/, *vous souteniez* /vu sutənje/ (contrast *vous soutenez* /vu sutne/), *nous ferions* /nu fərjɔ̃/ (contrast *nous ferons* /nu frɔ̃/), *vous seriez* /vu sərje/ (contrast *vous serez* /vu sre/), *il n'a envie de rien* /il na ɑ̃vi də rjɛ̃/.

Fouché (1969: 100) also advocates the pronunciation /ə/ before /lɥ/, /rɥ/ and /rw/, but in practice the mute *e* is often dropped in such circumstances, e.g. *essai de lui écrire* /ese d lɥi ekri:r/, *pas de ruisseau* /pɑ d rɥiso/, *il n'y a pas de roi* /il ni a pɑ d rwa/ (but /ə/ is not dropped in *celui*, e.g. *je prends celui-ci* /ʒə prɑ̃ səlɥi si/; note however that in familiar pronunciation *celui* often becomes /sɥi/, e.g. *celui-là* /sɥi la/). No such restriction applies before /nɥ/, e.g. *pas de nuage* /pɑ d nɥa:ʒ/, *rien de nuisible* /rjɛ̃ d nɥizibl/.

11.6.3   It will not usually shock the ear of a native-speaker of French if the /ə/ is pronounced in the case of (i) mono-syllables, e.g. *vous le verrez* /vu lə vɛre/, (ii) the initial syllable of a word, e.g. *vous venez* /vu vəne/, *la semaine* /la səmɛn/. Indeed, Henriette Walter comments (1990: 29) that 'de nos jours, les prononciations *des ch'minées, très m'suré, qui d'vait, la f'melle, est r'connu, il m'a r'mis* sont plus rares que *des cheminées, très mesuré, qui devait, la femelle, est reconnu, il m'a remis*'.

11.6.4   Rule 3 should always be applied in the case of a mute *e* occurring in a syllable other than the initial syllable (except of course in the circumstances noted in 11.6.2): it is not at all usual to pronounce the mute *e* in such words as *all(e)mand* /almã/, *app(e)lez-moi* /aple mwa/, *bouch(e)rie* /buʃri/, *(je) chant(e)rai* /ʃãtre/, *dang(e)reux* /dãʒrø/, *jug(e)ment* /ʒyʒmã/, *lent(e)ment* /lãtmã/, *longu(e)ment* /lõgmã/, *sam(e)di* /samdi/.

11.7   Rule 4

Rule 4: within a group, mute *e* is generally pronounced if it is preceded by two or more pronounced consonants.

11.7.1   Apart from the exceptions noted in 11.7.2 and 11.7.3, the rule is always applied.

On the reduction of the clusters /tr/, /bl/, etc., to /t/, /b/, etc., when followed by mute *e*, see 11.10 and 16.5.3.

11.7.2   The point was made in 7.4 that, as a phonetic entity, the word has no real existence in French. This is entirely true in the sense that there are no clues within a group that would enable one to determine where one word ends and the next begins. On the other hand, the speaker's awareness that a string of sounds that he or she is uttering consists of more than one word may in certain circumstances condition his or her pronunciation. In particular, rule 4 often does not apply when a mute *e at the end of a word* is preceded by two consonants but followed (i.e. at the beginning of the next word) by only one consonant, e.g. *il parl(e) beaucoup* /il parl boku/, *la forc(e) de frappe* /la fɔrs də frap/.

It has been shown (Dauzes, 1973: 48) that the /ə/ is more likely to be retained when the syllable immediately following takes a main stress than when it does not, e.g. *c'est un texte court* /sɛt œ̃ tɛkstə kuːr/, *il reste là* /il rɛstə la/, *une porte verte* /yn pɔrtə vɛrt/, but *c'est un texte connu* /sɛt œ̃ tɛkst kɔny/, *il reste couché* /il rɛst kuʃe/, *une porte fermée* /yn pɔrt fɛrme/ – but this is a tendency, not a rule, and pronunciations such as /yn pɔrt vɛrt/ are perfectly possible.

Note that the tendency to drop the *e* does not in any case apply to *quelque(s)*, e.g. *quelque distance* /kɛlkə distɑ̃ːs/, *quelques jours* /kɛlkə ʒuːr/.

11.7.3   At the end of the first part of compound words such as *garde-boue*, *porte-monnaie*, the mute *e* is normally pronounced if the second part is a monosyllable, e.g. *garde-boue* /gardəbu/, *porte-clefs* /pɔrtəkle/, *porte-plume* /pɔrtəplym/, but is frequently (though not invariably) dropped when the second part has more than one syllable, e.g. *gard(e)-barrière* /gardbarjɛːr/, *port(e)-monnaie* /pɔrtmɔnɛ/ (compare 11.7.2).

11.7.4   So strong is the tendency to pronounce a mute *e* after a cluster of two consonants that one may be introduced even when there is no corresponding *e* in writing. This is particularly true of *(un) ours blanc* /ursə blɑ̃/ and *(un) ours brun* /ursə brœ̃/, but it may sometimes occur elsewhere, e.g. *l'ex-roi* /lɛksərwa/, *(un) film muet* /filmə mɥe/ for the more usual /lɛksrwa/, /film mɥɛ/.

11.8   Three or More Mute *e*s in Succession

When there are more than three syllables in succession each having a mute *e*, the above rules can be applied, apart from the exceptions noted: i.e., when only one consonant precedes, the *e* is not pronounced, but when more than one consonant precedes, it is, e.g. *je l(e) devine* /ʒə l dəvin/, *je n(e) le r(e)garde pas* /ʒə n lə rgard pɑ/, *c'est c(e) que j(e) demandais* /sɛ s kə ʒ dəmɑ̃dɛ/, *c'est c(e) que j(e) te d(e)mandais* /sɛ s kə ʒ tə dmɑ̃dɛ/.

However, in general it is probably true to say that the more mute *e*s there are in succession, the greater the likelihood that some at least of them will be pronounced even when the option of dropping them exists. To be on the safe side, the foreign learner is well advised to pronounce the third and later instances of mute *e* in a succession (e.g. *tu n(e) le regardes pas* /ty n lə rəgard pɑ/) except in contexts where experience has shown that it is usual to drop them.

11.9   Miscellaneous Points

11.9.1   Pronounced mute *e* occurs in hiatus with a following vowel in certain circumstances, of which the following are the most frequent:

(i) before the so-called 'aspirate *h*' (i.e. an *h* that used to be pronounced but is so no longer), e.g. *le houx* /lə u/, *dehors* /dəɔːr/, *ils le haïssent* /il lə ais/, *beaucoup de haricots* /boku də ariko/, *il ne hurle pas* /il nə yrl pɑ/, and usually, in such circumstances, at the end of monosyllables such as *une, cette, grande, belle*, e.g. *une honte* /ynə ɔ̃ːt/, *cette hâte* /sɛtə ɑːt/, *une grande haine* /yn grɑ̃də ɛn/, *la belle haie* /la bɛlə ɛ/; however, the /ə/ is not usually pronounced with *être* and *faire*, e.g. *être haï* /ətr ai/, *faire halte* /fɛr alt/, or at the end of words of two or more syllables, e.g. *la culture hollandaise* /la kyltyr ɔlɑ̃dɛːz/

(ii) before *onze, onzième*, e.g. *le onze mars* /lə ɔ̃z mars/, *plus de onze* /ply də ɔ̃:z/, *il n'en a que onze* /il nɑ̃ n a kə ɔ̃:z/, *le tome onze* /lə tɔmə ɔ̃:z/, *le onzième jour* /lə ɔ̃zjɛm ʒu:r/; but note that before the expression *onze heures* meaning 'eleven o'clock' the mute *e* may be either pronounced or not, e.g. (*il est*) *presque onze heures* /prɛsk ɔ̃z œ:r/ or /prɛskə ɔ̃z œ:r/, (*à partir*) *d'onze heures* /dɔ̃z œ:r/ or (*à partir*) *de onze heures* /də ɔ̃z œ:r/

(iii) before *un* meaning 'the number 1', e.g. *compter de un à dix* /kɔ̃te də œ̃ a dis/, *entre un et six* /ətrə œ̃ e sis/; note the difference between (*j'*)*en demande un*, (*il*) *en demande un*, (*ils*) *en demandent un* /ɑ̃ dmɑ̃də œ̃/ meaning '(I am, he is, they are) asking for *one* [i.e. just one, not more than one]' and (*j'*)*en demand(e) un*, (*il*) *en demand(e) un*, (*ils*) *en demand(ent) un* /ɑ̃ dmɑ̃d œ̃/ meaning '(I am, he is, they are) asking for one (of them)' (i.e. with no emphasis on 'one').

11.9.2   In conventional usage, there is a widespread tendency for clusters consisting of a stop or /v/ + /r/ or /l/ followed by mute *e* at the end of a word, e.g. *notre, impossible*, to lose their second consonant, /r/ or /l/, when immediately followed within the same stress-group by a word beginning with a consonant, e.g. *not(re) maison* /nɔt mɛzɔ̃/ for /nɔtrə mɛzɔ̃/, *impossib(le) d'y aller* /ɛ̃pɔsib di ale/ for /ɛ̃pɔsiblə di ale/, *une liv(re) de pommes* /yn liv də pɔm/; for more on this, see 16.5.3.

12 Vowel Length

12.1 Introduction

12.1.1 As in all languages, the vowels of French vary in length, in the sense that, whether one is speaking quickly or slowly, some are longer than others. Such variations in length may or may not be significant and, if they are not, the native-speaker may not even be aware of them: for instance, how many native-speakers of English are conscious of the fact that they use a longer vowel in such words as *leave*, *ease*, *feed* than in such words as *leaf*, *cease*, *feet*? But it is important for a non-native-speaker to get it right: if a foreigner whose accent is in other respects impeccable pronounces *leaf*, *cease*, *feet* with the slightly longer vowel of *leave*, *ease*, *feed*, a native-speaker will recognize that something is not quite right even if he or she is not necessarily able to identify just what it is about the foreigner's pronunciation that sounds wrong.

12.1.2 In discussing the length of vowels in French, we have to consider (i) in what circumstances vowels can be long (12.3–12.7) and (ii) whether or not the difference between short and long vowels is ever significant (or distinctive, or phonemic) (12.8).

12.1.3 In practice, we shall need to consider only two degrees of length that, for simplicity, we can call 'short' and 'long'. In reality, there are at least four degrees of length in French. Carton, for example, points out (1974: 42) that (assuming the words in question are all stressed) the vowel of *dort* is longer than that of *doge*, which is longer than that of *dogue*, which is itself longer than that of *dot*. If one wanted to be very subtle, and if different degrees of length were indicated by [::], [:] and [·] respectively, we could represent this series of words as follows:

dɔ::r   dɔ:ʒ   dɔ·g   dɔt

For our purposes, we can (like most other books on French pronunciation) ignore the fact that the vowel of *doge* is slightly shorter than that of *dort* and that the vowel of *dogue* is slightly longer than that of *dot*. For practical purposes, we can consider that the vowel of stressed *dort* and *doge* is long and that the vowel of *dogue* and *dot* is short.

12.1.4 *Note that vowel length is indicated by a colon*, e.g. /dɔ:r/, /dɔ:ʒ/, but /dɔg/, /dɔt/.

12.2 Five Simple Rules

The rules for vowel length in French are few and simple:

1 All unstressed vowels are short (12.3).
2 All stressed vowels in open syllables are short (12.4).
3 The vowels /ø/, /o/ and /ɑ/ and the nasal vowels are always long when stressed and in a closed syllable (12.5).
4 All other vowels are long when stressed and in a closed syllable ending in /v/, /z/, /ʒ/, /r/ or /vr/ (12.6).
5 In other stressed closed syllables, these other vowels are short (12.7).

Rules 3, 4 and 5 are illustrated below (12.5 to 12.7) with reference to syllables having normal stress (9.4). Practice in respect of vowel length in syllables taking an emphatic stress (9.5) or a contrastive stress (9.6) varies according to the degree and type of stress and from one individual to another but, in general, if the same rules are applied as in the case of syllables having normal stress, the results will be acceptable.

12.3 Rule 1

All unstressed vowels are short, e.g. *Qu'est-ce vous cherchez?* /kɛs kə vu ʃɛrˈʃe/, *vous ne connaissez pas mon fils* /vu n kɔnɛse pɑ mɔ̃ ˈfis/, *j'aime beaucoup | la cuisine espagnole* /ʒɛm boˈku | la kɥizin ɛspaˈɲɔl/.

12.4 Rule 2

All stressed vowels in open syllables are short, e.g. the final syllables of such words and phrases as the following, even when stressed: *j'ai fini* /ʒe fiˈni/, *la beauté* /la boˈte/, *tout à fait* /tut a ˈfɛ/, *voilà!* /vwaˈla/, *je l'ai vu* /ʒə le ˈvy/, *un peu* /œ̃ ˈpø/, *partout* /parˈtu/, *il est beau* /il ɛ ˈbo/, *je ne peux pas* /ʒə n pø ˈpɑ/, *très bien* /trɛ ˈbjɛ̃/, *aucun* /oˈkœ̃/, *la façon* /la faˈsɔ̃/, *c'est trop grand* /sɛ tro ˈgrɑ̃/.

12.5 Rule 3

The vowels /ø/, /o/, /ɑ/ and the nasal vowels /ɛ̃/, /œ̃/, /ɔ̃/ and /ɑ̃/ are always long when stressed and in a closed syllable, e.g. (in stressed contexts) *neutre* /ˈnø:tr/, *joyeuse* /ʒwaˈjø:z/, *le nôtre* /lə ˈno:tr/, *la Gaule* /la ˈgo:l/, *ma faute* /ma ˈfo:t/, *les pâtes* /le ˈpɑ:t/, *le sable* /lə ˈsɑ:bl/, *enceinte* /ɑ̃ˈsɛ̃:t/, *vaincre* /ˈvɛ̃:kr/, *le singe* /lə ˈsɛ̃:ʒ/, *humble* /ˈœ̃:bl/, *j'emprunte* /ʒɑ̃ˈprœ̃:t/, *la honte* /la ˈɔ̃:t/, *le songe* /lə ˈsɔ̃:ʒ/, *onze* /ˈɔ̃:z/, *elle est grande* /ɛl ɛ ˈgrɑ̃:d/, *la France* /la ˈfrɑ̃:s/, *une tranche* /yn ˈtrɑ̃:ʃ/.

12.6 Rule 4

Other vowels, i.e. /i/, /ɛ/, /a/, /y/, /œ/, /u/ and /ɔ/, are long when stressed and in a closed syllable ending in /v/, /z/, /ʒ/, /r/ or /vr/, e.g. (in stressed contexts) *rive* /ˈriːv/, *les assises* /lez aˈsiːz/, *noblesse oblige* /nɔblɛs ɔˈbliːʒ/, *partir* /parˈtiːr/, *ivre* /ˈiːvr/, *brève* /ˈbrɛːv/, *à l'aise* /a ˈlɛːz/, *que sais-je?* /kə ˈsɛːʒ/, *fièvre* /ˈfjɛːvr/, *cave* /ˈkaːv/, *image* /iˈmaːʒ/, *rare* /ˈraːr/, *cadavre* /kaˈdaːvr/, *étuve* /eˈtyːv/, *il refuse* /il rəˈfyːz/, *refuge* /rəˈfyːʒ/, *impur* /ɛ̃ˈpyːr/, *bonheur* /bɔˈnœːr/, *veuve* /ˈvœːv/, *œuvre* /ˈœːvr/, *je trouve* /ʒə ˈtruːv/, *il bouge* /il ˈbuːʒ/, *j'ouvre* /ˈʒuːvr/, *Limoges* /liˈmɔːʒ/, *sort* /ˈsɔːr/, *Hanovre* /aˈnɔːvr/.

Notes: (i) The 'lengthening consonants' /v/, /z/, /ʒ/ and /r/ are all voiced fricatives. (ii) Clusters of two voiced fricatives other than /vr/ do *not* cause lengthening, e.g. *larve* /ˈlarv/, *conserve* /kɔ̃ˈsɛrv/, *berge* /ˈbɛrʒ/, *large* /ˈlarʒ/, *Panurge* /paˈnyrʒ/, *forge* /ˈfɔrʒ/, *quatorze* /kaˈtɔrz/. (iii) The vowel /e/ does not occur in closed syllables (see 10.6.2). (iv) The vowel /ə/ is never stressed (see 11.1.2 (ii)).

12.7 Rule 5

In other stressed closed syllables, the vowels /i/, /ɛ/, /a/, /y/, /œ/, /u/ and /ɔ/ are short (but see 12.8), e.g. *vide* /ˈvid/, *vite* /ˈvit/, *vitre* /ˈvitr/, *cime* /ˈsim/, *signe* /ˈsiɲ/, *filtre* /ˈfiltr/, (*ils*) *finissent* /fiˈnis/, *riche* /ˈriʃ/, *laide* /ˈlɛd/, *pêche* /ˈpɛʃ/, *cercle* /ˈsɛrkl/, *svelte* /ˈsvɛlt/, *auberge* /oˈbɛrʒ/, *parade* /paˈrad/, *platane* /plaˈtan/, *montagne* /mɔ̃ˈtaɲ/, *vaste* /ˈvast/, (*ils*) *partent* /ˈpart/, *Chartres* /ˈʃartr/, *tube* /ˈtyb/, *costume* /kɔsˈtym/, *urge* /ˈyrʒ/, *club* /ˈklœb/, *bœuf* /ˈbœf/, *seul* /ˈsœl/, *jeune* /ˈʒœn/, *foule* /ˈful/, *boom* /ˈbum/, (*il*) *tousse* /ˈtus/, *farouche* /faˈruʃ/, *boucle* /ˈbukl/, *féroce* /feˈrɔs/, *orge* /ˈɔrʒ/, *code* /ˈkɔd/, *globe* /ˈglɔb/, *torse* /ˈtɔrs/, *porte* /ˈpɔrt/.

12.8 Is Vowel Length Ever Phonemic in French?

12.8.1 If the indications given above are followed consistently, the results in respect of vowel length will always be acceptable. There are, however, certain words in which an alternative pronunciation is possible. More specifically, certain words that, according to rule 5 (12.7), would have a short vowel *may* also be pronounced with a long vowel, e.g. *maître* /mɛtr/ or /mɛ:tr/.

12.8.2 This feature affects exclusively (or almost exclusively – see 12.8.3) the vowel /ɛ/, and, of course, only when it is in a closed syllable and takes a main stress.

Some speakers certainly do, at least on occasion, make a distinction between, say, *mettre* /ˈmɛtr/ and *maître* /ˈmɛ:tr/. In so far as such a distinction does exist, one has to recognize that it is phonemic, i.e. that /ɛ/ and /ɛ:/ count as separate phonemes. The number of pairs in which it even *can* occur is very small, and may well be limited to the following:

/ɛ/		/ɛ:/	
belle	/bɛl/	*bêle*	/bɛ:l/
bette	/bɛt/	*bête*	/bɛ:t/
elle	/ɛl/	*aile*	/ɛ:l/
faite	/fɛt/	*fête*	/fɛ:t/
laide	/lɛd/	*l'aide*	/lɛ:d/
lettre	/lɛtr/	*l'être*	/lɛ:tr/
mettre	/mɛtr/	*maître*	/mɛ:tr/
saine	/sɛn/	*scène, Seine*	/sɛ:n/
tette	/tɛt/	*tête*	/tɛ:t/

It must be pointed out, however, that the majority of French speakers do not observe the distinction and, in so far as it exists at all, it tends to be characteristic of the speech of the older generation (it is, says Henriette Walter, 1977: 43, 'd'autant moins vivant que le sujet est plus jeune'). Furthermore, few (if any) speakers observe it in all the above pairs. In the circumstances, there is no need whatsoever for foreigners to make any effort to observe the distinction.

12.8.3 It is sometimes claimed that a similar distinction exists between (*je*, *il*) *tousse* /ˈtus/ and the pronoun *tous* /ˈtuːs/. The pronunciation *tous* [tuːs] *can* be heard when the word is subject to emphatic stress, but this is a feature of little significance that can be safely ignored.

12.9 Other Alternatives

Other departures from the indications given under rules 4 and 5 above may well be heard in French as spoken by educated Parisians, such as a short vowel before /v/ or /ʒ/ (e.g. *veuve* /ˈvœv/, *rouge* /ˈruʒ/) or a long vowel before the voiced stops /b/, /d/ and /g/ or voiced clusters such as /bl/, e.g. *robe* /ˈrɔːb/, *vide* /ˈviːd/, *vogue* /ˈvɔːg/, *table* /ˈtaːbl/, but these too can safely be ignored and indeed, to be on the safe side, are best not imitated.

13 The Semi-Consonants in Detail

13.1 Introduction

Of the three semi-consonants of French, only one, viz. /j/, can occur between vowels (as in *payer* /peje/) or after a vowel (as in *œil* /œj/) (see 5.1.3). Note that /j/ is often referred to as 'yod' (a name derived from that of a letter of the Hebrew alphabet).

13.2 /i/ or /j/ after a Vowel?

There are a very few words (e.g. *abbaye* /abei/) in which the vowel /i/ is in hiatus with a preceding vowel. Some of these differ only in that single respect from other words ending in /j/:

haï	/ai/	*ail, aïe*	/aj/
pays	/pɛi/ or more normally /pei, peji/	*paye*	/pɛj/

13.3 /j/, /l/ or /ll/ after /i/?

13.3.1 No simple all-embracing rules can be given for the pronunciation of -*ll*- after /i/, but the following indications cover most cases (on /ll/ and on geminated consonants in general, see chapter 17):

13.3.2 At the beginning of a word, the pronunciation is usually /ill/ when the prefix has a negative value, e.g. *illégal* /illegal/, *illisible* /illizibl/, *illogique* /illɔʒik/, and in various other words (especially relatively uncommon or technical words), e.g. *illuminer* /illymine/, *illustre* /illystr/, *illuvial* /illyvjal/, but frequently /il/ in some relatively common words such as *illusion* /ilyzjɔ̃/, *illustrer* /ilystre/; the pronunciation is never /ij/ in this position.

13.3.3 Most verbs in *-iller* and derivatives thereof have /j/, e.g. *gaspiller* /gaspije/, *habiller* /abije/, *scintiller* /sɛ̃tije/, *vaciller* /vasije/ (occasionally /vasile/), but *distiller, instiller, osciller* are /distile, ɛ̃stile, ɔsile/; as for *titiller*, the pronunciation /titille/ or /titile/ is prescribed by most standard reference books, but it appears that, in practice, this verb is usually pronounced /titije/ (Martinet and Walter, 1973: 865).

13.3.4 Among relatively common words (for uncommon words, see Fouché, 1969: 311), the following and their derivatives have the pronunciation /il/: *mille* /mil/, *tranquille* /trɑ̃kil/, *ville* /vil/, and the proper name *Gilles* /ʒil/.

13.3.5 Most other words in relatively common use have /ij/, e.g. *artillerie* /artijri/, *bille* /bij/, *billet* /bijɛ/, *fille* /fij/, *fillette* /fijɛt/, *quille* /kij/, *rillettes* /rijɛt/, *sillon* /sijɔ̃/, and their derivatives; also the name of the poet *Villon* /vijɔ̃/ (occasionally /vilɔ̃/).

13.4 Intervocalic /j/

13.4.1 Intervocalic /j/ is represented in spelling by *y*, *ï*, *ill* (or, after *i*, by *ll* – see 13.3.3 and 13.3.5), e.g:

(*nous*) *ayons*	/ɛjɔ̃/	*aïeul*	/ajœl/	*ensoleillé*	/ɑ̃sɔlɛje/
ennuyeux	/ɑ̃nɥijø/	*païen*	/pajɛ̃/	*paillasse*	/pajas/
moyen	/mwajɛ̃/			*souillon*	/sujɔ̃/
payer	/peje/			*veuillez*	/vœje/

13.4.2 What happens when intervocalic /j/, represented either by *y* (as in *payer*) or by *ill* (as in *travailler*), is followed by one or other of the endings -*ions* /jɔ̃/ or -*iez* /je/, in either the present subjunctive or the imperfect indicative? In careful speech the result is a long or geminate (see chapter 17) form of the semi-consonant, represented as /jj/, e.g. (*nous*) *employions* /ɑ̃plwajjɔ̃/, *travaillions* /travajjɔ̃/, *cueillions* /kœjjɔ̃/, (*vous*) *payiez* /pɛjje/, *croyiez* /krwajje/, *asseyiez* /assɛjje/, but in colloquial speech the pronunciation of such forms is usually identical to that of the forms of the present indicative, *employons*, *travaillons*, *cueillons*, *payez*, *croyez*, *asseyez*, etc., viz. /ɑ̃plwajɔ̃, travajɔ̃, kœjɔ̃, peje, krwaje, asɛje/.

13.4.3 A /j/ is normally inserted in pronunciation, but is not represented in spelling, between the vowel /i/ and an immediately following vowel, e.g. *février* /fevrije/, *client* /klijɑ̃/, *crier* /krije/, *quatrième* /katrijɛm/. Such a 'transitional vowel' may also occur between /e/ or /ɛ/ and /i/ in *abbaye* /abeji, abɛji/, *pays* /peji, pɛji/.

13.5 /ɥ/

13.5.1 It is important for the foreign learner to distinguish clearly between the semi-consonants /ɥ/ and /w/. The main difficulty is not just that /ɥ/ is a characteristically French sound but that it seems to have no equivalent in any other European language, or indeed any other well-known language. The tendency for native-speakers of English as of many other languages is to substitute for it a /w/-type sound.

13.5.2 The most satisfactory way of acquiring the sound is perhaps first to pronounce the vowel /u/ and convert it into

the consonant /w/ and then, by a similar process, to pronounce the vowel /y/ and, while taking care not to change the
position of the tongue or lips, convert *that* into a semi-
consonant. There should be no great difficulty about achieving
a satisfactory result, particularly if a native-speaker of French
can be consulted.

13.5.3 It is important to make the effort to pronounce /ɥ/
correctly since it in fact occurs very widely in French, e.g., to
take a selection of words in which it is followed by a range of
different vowels, *huit* /ɥit/, *tuer* /tɥe/, *Suède* /sɥɛd/, *nuage*
/nɥaːʒ/, *lueur* /lɥœːr/, *juin* /ʒɥɛ̃/, *tuons* /tɥɔ̃/, *nuance*
/nɥãːs/.

13.6   /ɥ/ and /w/

The importance of the distinction between /ɥ/ and /w/ can be
judged from the fact that there are several 'minimal pairs', i.e.
pairs of words distinguished only by the fact that one has /ɥ/
and the other /w/, e.g.:

	/ɥ/		/w/
s'enfuir	/sãfɥiːr/	*s'enfouir*	/sãfwiːr/
juin	/ʒɥɛ̃/	*joint*	/ʒwɛ̃/
lui	/lɥi/	*Louis*	/lwi/
luise	/lɥiːz/	*Louise*	/lwiːz/
muette	/mɥɛt/	*mouette*	/mwɛt/
nuée	/nɥe/	*noué*	/nwe/
sua	/sɥa/	*soi*, *soit*	/swa/
tua	/tɥa/	*toi*, *toit*	/twa/

13.7   Vowel or Semi-Consonant?

13.7.1 We now have to address the problem of words such
as *lien*, *prier*, *tueur*, *truand*, *jouet*, *prouesse*, and decide

whether *i*, *u*, *ou* before a vowel represent /i, y, u/ or the corresponding semi-consonants /j, ɥ, w/. If the indications in 13.7.2–13.7.7 are followed, no problems of consequence are likely to arise.

13.7.2   In initial position (i.e. when no consonant precedes), use the semi-consonant, e.g:

hiérarchie	/jerarʃi/	*huer*	/ɥe/	*ouate*	/wat/
iambe	/jãːb/	*Huon*	/ɥɔ̃/	*ouest*	/wɛst/
iode	/jɔd/			*ouïr*	/wiːr/

13.7.3   When only one consonant precedes, either at the beginning or in the middle of a word, the usual pronunciation is a semi-consonant, e.g.:

alliance	/aljãːs/	*duodénum*	/dɥɔdenɔm/	*douane*	/dwan/
confiant	/kɔ̃fjã/	*lingual*	/lɛ̃gɥal/	*échouer*	/eʃwe/
diabète	/djabɛt/	*lueur*	/lɥœːr/	*fouet*	/fwɛ/
épicier	/episje/	*muet*	/mɥɛ/	(*nous*) *louons*	/lwɔ̃/
janvier	/ʒãvje/	*nuage*	/nɥaːʒ/	*Louis*	/lwi/
lion	/ljɔ̃/	*ruelle*	/rɥɛl/	*nouer*	/nwe/
nier	/nje/	*suave*	/sɥaːv/	*Rouen*	/rwã/
pieux	/pjø/	*Suède*	/sɥɛd/	*souhait*	/swɛ/
sciure	/sjyːr/	*sueur*	/sɥœːr/	*tatouer*	/tatwe/
viande	/vjãːd/	*tuer*	/tɥe/	*vouer*	/vwe/

13.7.4   In certain words that would normally be covered by the principles set out in 13.7.2 and 13.7.3, and particularly when the group consonant + semi-consonant occurs at the beginning of the word, a vowel rather than a semi-consonant not infrequently occurs, especially in rather slow speech and/or after a word ending in a consonant. In such cases, /i/ is followed by a transitional /j/ (see 13.4.3), e.g. *lion* /lijɔ̃/, *une liaison* /yn lijɛzɔ̃/; also *nuage* /nyaːʒ/, *nouer* /nue/, etc.

In some words, the pronunciation with a vowel is in fact the more usual, e.g. *hier* /ijɛːr/ or /jɛːr/, *riant*, which is nearly always /rijã/, and *buanderie*, for which Martinet and Walter (1973) give only the pronunciation /byãdri/.

13.7.5   After a consonant cluster consisting of a stop, /f/ or /v/ + /l/ or /r/, the pronunciation is a vowel not a semi-consonant, e.g.:

cendrier /sãdrije/	*affluence* /aflyã:s/	*clouer* /klue/
février /fevrije/	*cruel* /kryɛl/	*éblouissant* /ebluisã/
(*il*) *oublia* /ublija/	*fluorure* /flyɔry:r/	*écrouer* /ekrue/
patriote /patrijɔt/	*truand* /tryã/	*trouer* /true/
plier /plije/		
(*je*) *priais* /prijɛ/		
quatrième /katrijɛm/		
triomphe /trijɔ̃:f/		

This does not apply to /ɥi/ (see 13.7.7) or to the spelling *oi* (see 13.7.8).

13.7.6   After other consonantal groups, the pronunciation is usually a semi-consonant, e.g:

dernier /dɛrnje/	*actuel* /aktɥɛl/	*escouade* /ɛskwad/
espion /ɛspjɔ̃/	*estuaire* /ɛstɥɛ:r/	
forestier /fɔrestje/	*éternuer* /etɛrnɥe/	
gardien /gardjɛ̃/	*fastueux* /fastɥø/	
partiel /parsjɛl/	*Stuart* /stɥa:r/	
quartier /kartje/		

13.7.7   The group *ui* is always pronounced /ɥi/, even after a group stop or /f/ + /l/ or /r/ (see 13.7.5), e.g. *bruit* /brɥi/, *construire* /kɔ̃strɥi:r/, *fluide* /flɥid/, *fruit* /frɥi/, *truite* /trɥit/.

13.7.8   The group *oi* (*oî*) is always pronounced /wa/ or /wɑ/ (see 10.9.4), even after a stop or /f/ + /l/ or /r/ (see 13.7.5), e.g. *Blois* /blwa/, *cloison* /klwazɔ̃/, *croire* /krwa:r/, *droit* /drwɑ/, *effroi* /efrwɑ/, *étroit* /etrwɑ/, *gloire* /glwa:r/, *trois* /trwɑ, trwa/ (contrast *troua* /trua/).

14 The Consonants in Detail: (I) Stops

14.1 Introduction

14.1.1 French has what can be considered, with a fair amount of justification, as the same six stops (see 6.3.1) as English: viz.:

  (i) the voiceless and voiced bilabial stops, /p/ and /b/
 (ii) the voiceless and voiced dental (or, in English, alveolar – see 14.4.2) stops, /t/ and /d/
(iii) the voiceless and voiced velar stops, /k/ and /g/.

14.1.2 However, though the two languages have the same inventory of phonemes in this respect, and though anyone who uses the English stops when speaking French will usually be understood without difficulty, there are several significant differences in the way French and English stops are articulated, so much so that an English stop is rarely if ever identical with its French equivalent.

14.2 Mode of Articulation (General)

14.2.1 The utterance of a stop normally involves three stages, viz.:

(i) the **closing** or **implosion**, i.e. the stage at which the flow of air is stopped at (to consider only the stops of French and English) the lips (/p/ and /b/), the teeth or alveoli (/t/, /d/), or the velum (/k/, /g/); this stage is sometimes referred to as 'closure', but since this term is also used with reference not to the 'act of closing', i.e. stage (i), but to the 'period of closure', i.e. stage (ii), it is perhaps better avoided

(ii) the **holding** stage during which the air is held in a state of compression (the term 'compression' is sometimes used for this stage) behind the point of articulation

(iii) the **release** or **explosion**, i.e. the stage at which the pent-up air is released and an audible 'explosion' is created.

14.2.2   As we have seen (6.4), the vocal cords may or may not be vibrating during the production of a consonant; a consonant (or segment of a consonant) that is accompanied by vibration of the vocal cords is voiced, one that is not is voiceless.

14.2.3   In discussing the most significant differences between French and English stops, we have to take account both of the different stages referred to in 14.2.1 and of the voiced–voiceless opposition.

14.3   French and English Stops

14.3.1   In the English of most native-speakers (though not necessarily all) the release of voiceless stops, particularly at the beginning of a word, is accompanied by a puff of air – this can be felt if you put the back of your hand an inch or so in front of your mouth and say *pin* or *pool* or *pie* or some other word beginning with /p/ (it is less noticeable in the case of words beginning with /t/ or /k/, but it is there). This is known as **aspiration** and so we can say that voiceless stops in English are **aspirated**. If we represent this by a superscript [ʰ], we can transcribe *pin*, *pool* as [pʰɪn], [pʰuːl]. French voiceless consonants, however, are not aspirated and native-speakers of English should make a conscious effort to avoid using aspirated stops when speaking French.

Unaspirated stops do occur in English, particularly after /s/ – if you hold the back of your hand in front of your mouth (as for *pin* above) and say *spin*, you will not feel a puff of air. (An alternative method of demonstrating the existence or otherwise of aspiration is to hold a lighted match an inch or so in front of the mouth and say *pin* – this should blow the match out, whereas if you say *spin*, you will probably not blow it out.) There is also little or no aspiration when an intervocalic consonant follows the stressed vowel, as in *supper*.

14.3.2 In final position, i.e. before a pause, as in *wake up!*, *good night*, *too bad*, *very big*, English stops may (but not necessarily) lack the last of the three stages referred to in 14.2.1, i.e. they are not 'released', the tongue remains for a while at the point of articulation. This is not the case in French and, in utterances such as *en Europe* /ɑ̃n ørɔp/, *j'aime ta robe* /ʒɛm ta rɔb/, *vite* /vit/, *c'est vide* /sɛ vid/, *j'ai le trac* /ʒe l trak/, *c'est trop vague* /sɛ tro vag/, care must be taken to ensure that the consonant is released.

14.3.3 Whereas the initial stops of English words such as *boy*, *day*, *gone*, and the final stops of words such as *rob*, *fad*, *fig*, are only partially voiced, in French the initial stops of words such as *boue*, *dos*, *goût*, and the final stops of words such as *robe*, *fade*, *figue*, are fully voiced throughout (see 6.4.4). Indeed if anything the voicing in words such as *robe*, etc., may continue after the release has taken place, with the result that one sometimes hears a fleeting [ə]-sound after the consonant, e.g. [rɔbᵊ].

14.4   Point of Articulation

14.4.1   /p/, /b/

In both languages, /p/ and /b/ are bilabial stops, but whereas in English they are pronounced with the lips in a more or less relaxed neutral position (i.e. in the position they occupy when the mouth is closed in a normal way), in French the lips are to some extent pursued or protruded – this is connected with the fact that the articulation of French is characterized in general by much greater muscular tension than that of English (see 3.1).

14.4.2   /t/, /d/

The point of articulation in French is further forward than in English. In English, the tongue normally makes contact with the alveolar ridge behind the top teeth (see 2.5.2), but in French the point of articulation is the top teeth (though there is also contact with the front part of the alveoli, particularly in the case of /d/). The acoustic difference is slight but nevertheless noticeable. It may help native-speakers of English to produce a French-sounding /t/ or /d/ if they observe their own pronunciation of words or phrases in which /t/ or /d/ is followed immediately by /θ/ (voiceless *th*), e.g. *eighth* /eɪtθ/, at three /ət θri/, *width* /wɪdθ/, *a bad thing* /ə bæd θɪŋ/, in which context the point of articulation of /t/ and /d/ is the teeth (indeed, the point of articulation here may well be further forward than in the case of French /t/ and /d/).

14.4.3   /k/, /g/

These are generally classified as velar stops with reference to both English and French, but, in reality, in both languages the point of articulation varies according to what vowel follows. Before a back vowel such as those of English *cool*, *call*, *good*, *gone*, etc., contact is made between the back of the tongue and the back of the velum (or soft palate) but, before a front vowel such as that of English *keen*, *geese*, and even more so before a /j/ as in English *cube* /kju:b/, contact is made further forward, at the front of the velum and possibly the back of the palate as well.

In French, this tendency to anticipate the point of articulation of a following sound is even more marked than in English. So, while /k/ and /g/ have a velar articulation before or after a back vowel, as in *coup* /ku/, *goutte* /gut/, *côte* /ko:t/, *de Gaulle* /də go:l/, *cote* /kɔt/, *gorge* /gɔrʒ/, *câble* /kɑ:bl/, *roc* /rɔk/, *vogue* /vɔg/, the point of articulation is appreciably further forward before front vowels, particularly before /i/ and /y/, as in *qui* /ki/, *guide* /gid/, *cure* /ky:r/, *aigu* /egy/, and before the semi-consonant /ɥ/, as in *cuisse* /kɥis/, *aiguille* /egɥij/ – so much so that, in some people's pronunciation, what one hears is a palatal rather than a velar stop. Before other vowels, e.g. in words such as *quai* /ke/, *gué* /ge/, *quelle* /kɛl/, *guerre* /gɛ:r/, *quinze* /kɛ̃:z/, *gain* /gɛ̃/, *canne* /kan/, *garde* /gard/, the point of articulation is normally somewhere in between, i.e. well forward on the velum without however being as far forward as the palate.

14.5   A Canadianism

In Canadian French, the release of the dental stops /t/ and /d/ before the high front vowels /i/, /y/ or before the corresponding semi-consonants /j/, /ɥ/ is frequently accompanied by a fleeting [s]-sound (after voiceless /t/) or [z]-sound (after voiced /d/). This can be represented by a superscript [ˢ] or [ᶻ], e.g. *tirer* [tˢire], *type* [tˢɪp], *tu* [tˢʏ], *tube* [tˢʏb], *tiens* [tˢjɛ̃], *tuer* [tˢɥe], *dire* [dᶻi:r], *dû* [dᶻʏ], *reduire* [redᶻɥi:r]. (For the vowels [ɪ] and [ʏ], see 10.12.2.) (For more on this, see Walker, 1984: chapter 4, 'Canadian French Consonant System'.)

14.6   The Glottal Stop

The glottal stop (represented by the symbol [ʔ]) is the sound made by blocking the flow of air by closing the glottis or vocal cords and then releasing it. It occurs widely in English in three phonetic contexts (see 14.6.1–14.6.3) (and less widely in others that we shall not discuss).

14.6.1 In Cockney and Glasgow English, among others, it regularly occurs as a substitute for intervocalic /t/ (and sometimes /p/) in such words as *butter*, *daughter*, *letter*, *water*, *city*, *supper*. This must be avoided when speaking French, e.g. *petit* /pəti/.

14.6.2 It occurs very widely among English-speakers from many areas (including many who would not use it in *butter*, *letter*, etc. – see 14.6.1) as a substitute for /t/ as the end of a syllable and before another consonant, especially /n/, e.g. *frightening* /fraɪʔnɪŋ/, *neatness* /niːʔnɪs/, *treatment* /triːʔmənt/, *atmosphere* /æʔməsfɪə/, *settler* /seʔlə/, *catflap* /kæʔflæp/. This too must be carefully avoided in French, i.e. a normal /t/ *must* be used in words such as *atmosphère* /atmɔsfɛːr/, *ethnique* /ɛtnik/, *athlète* /atlɛt/.

14.6.3 A syllable beginning with a vowel is frequently introduced by a glottal stop, particularly:
   (i) at the beginning of a phrase, e.g. [ʔ]*afterwards*, [ʔ]*at any rate*, [ʔ]*early in the morning*
   (ii) when the vowel is in hiatus with a preceding vowel, e.g. *the* [ʔ]*end of the street*, *it won't be* [ʔ]*easy*, *she* [ʔ]*opened the door*
   (iii) for emphasis, e.g. *it's* [ʔ]*awful*, *at* [ʔ]*any time*, *I've* [ʔ]*only got one*, *What* [ʔ]*are you doing?*

14.6.4 In French, a glottal stop is sometimes used to introduce a syllable that bears an emphatic stress (see 9.5.2) and is not impossible elsewhere, but its use is much rarer than in English and it is best avoided altogether by foreigners except in cases of emphatic stress. Particular care should be taken to avoid introducing a glottal stop in contexts where two or more words are in hiatus, e.g. *Marie a acheté une robe* /mari a aʃte yn rɔb/, *nous allons à Amiens à onze heures* /nuz alɔ̃ a amjɛ̃ a ɔ̃z œːr/.

15 The Consonants in Detail: (II) Fricatives

15.1 French and English Fricatives

If we exclude /r/, which may or may not be a fricative depending upon which particular variety of it is adopted (see 16.1), French has six fricatives, all of them having corresponding but not necessarily identical phonemes in English, viz.:
  (i) the voiceless and voiced labio-dental fricatives, /f/ and /v/
 (ii) the voiceless and voiced dento-alveolar (see 15.3.2) fricatives, /s/ and /z/
(iii) the voiceless and voiced post-alveolar or pre-palatal (see 15.3.3) fricatives, /ʃ/ and /ʒ/.

15.2 Manner of Articulation

As in the case of the voiced stops (14.3.3), there is a tendency (which can vary extensively from speaker to speaker) in English for initial and final voiced fricatives to be only partially voiced (see 6.4.4). This must be avoided in French and a conscious effort made to ensure that the initial consonants of words such as *vite* /vit/, *zoo* /zo/, *jamais* /ʒamɛ/, and the final consonants of words such as *rive* /riːv/, *rose* /roːz/, *plage* /plaːʒ/, *large* /larʒ/, are fully voiced throughout. As in the case of the voiced stops (see 14.3.3), this is so strong a feature of French pronunciation that the voicing may even be prolonged after the articulation of a final consonant has ceased, with the result that the listener may sometimes detect a fleeting [ə]-sound, e.g. /roːzᵊ/, /larʒᵊ/.)

15.3   Point of Articulation

15.3.1   /f/, /v/

In both French and English, /f/ and /v/ are labio-dental fricatives, i.e. they are pronounced by forcing the air between the top teeth and the lower lip. Apart from the fact that, as with all consonants, the French varieties are pronounced with greater tension and energy than their English equivalents, there is no significant difference between the ways in which these consonants are pronounced in the two languages.

15.3.2   /s/ and /z/

Again, apart from the greater tension and energy characterizing the French varieties, there is little difference between the ways in which these phonemes are articulated in French and in English. In both languages, the point of articulation at which the audible friction occurs is between the tip or blade of the tongue and the alveoli. There is, however, a slight difference in that the tongue is generally somewhat flatter in the case of French than in the case of English. This effect can be achieved by positioning the tip of the tongue behind the lower teeth (and touching them), as is frequently the case with native-speakers in French.

15.3.3   /ʃ/, /ʒ/

These are variously known as post-alveolar, pre-palatal, alveo-palatal or palato-alveolar fricatives, a range of terms all of which serve to indicate that the point of articulation is between the blade of the tongue and the region of the roof of the mouth where the alveoli and the palate meet. If anything, the point of articulation in French is generally speaking slightly further forward (i.e. slightly less palatal) than in English. The most significant difference between the two languages, however, and the one that makes for an appreciable acoustic difference between the two, is the fact that French /ʃ/ and /ʒ/ are pronounced with the lips noticeably protruded and rounded. This is true not only when a rounded vowel follows or precedes, as in *chou* /ʃu/, *jour* /ʒuːr/, *chose* /ʃoːz/, *jaune* /ʒoːn/, *choc* /ʃɔk/, *jeu* /ʒø/, *jeune* /ʒœn/, *jonc* /ʒɔ̃/, *bouche* /buʃ/, *rouge* /ruːʒ/, *gauche* /goːʃ/, (*il*) *plonge* /plɔ̃ːʒ/, but also – if less so – in other positions, e.g. *chic* /ʃik/, *gîte* /ʒit/, *chez* /ʃe/, *chèvre* /ʃɛːvr/, (*je, il*) *jette* /ʒɛt/, *chat* /ʃa/, *jamais* /ʒamɛ/, *riche* /riʃ/, *tige* /tiːʒ/, *fraîche* /frɛʃ/, *ai-je* /ɛːʒ/, *tache* /taʃ/, *plage* /plaːʒ/, *acheter* /aʃte/, *à genoux* /a ʒnu/.

16 The Consonants in Detail: (III) /r/, /l/ and the Nasals

16.1 The Varieties of French /r/

16.1.1 At least three clearly distinguishable varieties of /r/ are used by different speakers of French but they do *not* include the /r/ that is characteristic of RP English (for 'RP', see 1.1.3). This is produced by allowing the air to escape between the tongue, which forms a groove (the shape of which varies according to the following vowel), and the alveoli. Generally speaking, there is no friction and, in the type of pronunciation in question, /r/ as in *red*, *reed*, *roe*, etc., can be considered a semi-consonant. This variety of /r/ must be avoided in French.

16.1.2 The /r/ sound that is generally characteristic of educated Parisian speech is pronounced by raising the back of the tongue towards the velum and the uvula. (One way of ensuring that it is the back of the tongue that is raised is to keep the tip of the tongue well down behind the bottom teeth). If the gap is narrow enough to create audible friction, then the result of course is a fricative consonant. (For reasons of simplicity, /r/ *is* classified as a velar fricative in the table in 6.11.) However, the gap may not be so narrow as to produce friction, in which case the consonant has an articulation more like that of a vowel (compare our remarks above, 16.1.1, on the non-fricative alveolar /r/ of English). Both varieties exist, and may well occur in the French of the same speaker depending upon the phonetic context (a fricative /r/ is more likely before a back vowel, for example, than before a front vowel). At all events, care should be taken to pronounce this variety of /r/ lightly, i.e. without an excessive amount of friction.

It might be noted that the point of articulation is not far removed from, but is further back than, that of /x/ (*ch*) of Scottish *loch*, German *Bach*, or the /x/ (*j*) of Spanish *hijo* – but, of course, French /r/ is normally voiced whereas /x/ is voiceless. Those who know Spanish (and know how to pronounce it correctly) might also note that this variety of French /r/ is not dissimilar to the Spanish voiced fricative [ɣ] of *pagar* [paɣar], *diga* [diɣa] (which is the voiced equivalent of /x/), except that, again, the point of articulation of the /r/ is further back.

16.1.3   Another 'back' variety of /r/ is produced by raising the back of the tongue, as for the fricative /r/ (see 16.1.2), and vibrating the uvula as in gargling. This 'rolled' variety, known in French as the '*r* grasseyé', is characteristic of some varieties of Parisian pronunciation. Anyone who has heard Edith Piaf sing, for example, '*Non, rien de rien, non, je ne regrette rien*', will have a very good idea of what it sounds like. As foreigners who attempt to use this form of /r/ often tend to overdo it, they are probably better advised to use the velar/uvular fricative /r/ described in 16.1.2 (which, in any case, is more widespread).

The -*r*- sound characteristic of the 'Northumberland burr' is a uvular rolled or fricative /r/.

16.1.4   A front rolled /r/, produced by vibrations of the tip of the tongue against the alveoli, in a rapid succession of taps, i.e. the kind of /r/ regularly heard in Scotland and Wales, also occurs extensively in French as spoken by people from many of the provinces. (It is also, incidentally, the /r/ recommended for use in singing.) It would certainly be acceptable for a foreigner whose spoken French is acquired in, say, Toulouse, and who has in general a southern accent, to use it, but, as it is not characteristic of French as spoken in Paris, it should be avoided by foreigners whose ambition it is to speak with a Parisian accent.

16.1.5   On voiceless [r̥], see 16.5.1.

16.2   The Lateral Consonant /l/

16.2.1   In English as spoken in the south of England there is a marked difference between /l/ as pronounced before a vowel, as in *leaf*, *life*, *loss*, *slog*, *please*, and /l/ as pronounced after a vowel, as in *all*, *feel*, *pool*, *old*, or at the end of a word after a stop, as in *bottle*, *middle*, *people*, *hobble*, *tickle*, *niggle*. The *l* that occurs before a vowel is known as a 'clear *l*' and the other as a 'dark *l*' (see 16.2.2) and it is important to appreciate the distinction since, though the clear *l* is not very different from a French *l*, the dark *l* is very different and must be avoided when speaking French.

The point of articulation for both clear *l* and dark *l* in English and for the French /l/ is the alveoli, i.e. the tip of the tongue touches the alveoli while the air escapes around the sides of the tongue (hence the term 'lateral'). The principal difference lies in the position of the remainder of the tongue (see 16.2.2).

16.2.2   For a clear *l*, the front of the tongue is raised towards, but does not touch, the palate. For a dark *l*, while the point of contact (between the tip of the tongue and the alveoli) is the same, the back of the tongue is raised at the same time towards the velum, in very much the same way as it is for the vowel /u/ or the /ʊ/ of *put* /pʊt/ or *loud* /laʊd/. In fact, if you say /u/ and, then, while modifying the position of the back of the tongue as little as possible, touch the alveoli with the tip of the tongue, you will produce a very markedly dark *l*. The dark *l* and the vowel /u/ or /ʊ/ do not sound very different from one another and, in Cockney English, an /ʊ/ sound (as in *put* /pʊt/) is often substituted for dark *l*, with the result that *milk*, *tell*, for example come to be pronounced [mɪʊk], [tɛʊ].

The important thing to remember is that a dark *l* is quite unacceptable in French, so much so that if words such as *ville*, *telle*, *foule*, *molle*, are pronounced with a *very* dark *l* they could be unintelligible. The French *l* is, if anything, rather 'clearer', i.e. pronounced with the front of the tongue raised somewhat closer to the palate, than the average English clear *l*, but the difference is minimal and the use of an English clear *l* is likely to pass more or less unnoticed.

16.2.3   Although, as mentioned above (16.2.1), the distinction between clear and dark *l* is characteristic of English as spoken in the south-east of England, this is not so of all varieties of English. In particular, Americans and Scots are likely to use a dark *l* (though not necessarily as dark a one as that of speakers from south-east England) in all positions, while English-speakers from Wales and Ireland may well use a clear *l* in all positions.

16.2.4   On voiceless [l̥], see 16.5.

16.3   The Nasal Consonants /m/, /n/, /ɲ/ and /ŋ/

16.3.1   The bilabial nasal /m/

Apart from the fact that, as in the case of other consonants, it is pronounced with greater tension, there is no significant difference in most phonetic contexts between the French /m/ and its English equivalent.

On voiceless [m̥], see 16.6.

16.3.2   The dental nasal /n/

Note that French /n/, like the stops /t/ and /d/ (see 14.4.2), is normally dental while English /n/, again like /t/ and /d/, is normally alveolar – i.e. the tip of the tongue makes contact with the teeth in French but with the alveoli in English. A dental [n] occurs in English, however, in words or phrases in which the consonant immediately precedes the dental fricative /θ/, e.g. *tenth*, *anthem*, *enthusiast*.

16.3.3   The palatal nasal /ɲ/

The point of articulation of this consonant, which does not exist in English, is the palate, i.e. the front of the tongue is raised until it touches the palate. There will be no difficulty in making contact in the right place if a conscious effort is made to ensure that the tip of the tongue is lowered, touching the bottom teeth, when pronouncing /ɲ/.

/ɲ/ is always written *gn*, and it occurs in only two positions, viz. either between vowels, as in *agneau* /aɲo/, *vignoble* /viɲɔbl/ (or very occasionally, between a vowel and the semi-consonant /j/, as in (*nous*) *peignions* /pɛɲjɔ̃/), or at the end of a word, as in *Allemagne* /almaɲ/, (*ils*) *peignent* /pɛɲ/, *vigne* /viɲ/.

It should be noted that /ɲ/ is *one* phoneme and that it is to be distinguished from the succession of two phonemes /nj/, as in French *union* /ynjɔ̃/ or (but pronounced with less tension) in English *union* /junjən/, *vineyard* /vɪnjəd/. That said, it must also be pointed out that there is an apparently increasing tendency for native-speakers of French to pronounce /nj/ instead of /ɲ/ in the intervocalic position, e.g. *agneau* /anjo/ for /aɲo/, and there is no good reason why this pronunciation should not be used by foreigners. But, at the end of a word, as in *Allemagne*, *peignent*, *vigne*, there is no acceptable alternative to /ɲ/.

16.3.4   The velar nasal /ŋ/

It is a moot point whether or not the sound /ŋ/, which is that of English *ng* in *ring*, etc., should be included in the inventory of French phonemes. It is true that it occurs almost exclusively (but see 18.3.4) in words ending in *-ing* borrowed from English, e.g. *building* /bildiŋ/, *meeting* /mitiŋ/, *parking*

/parkiŋ/, and that, in such words, some speakers substitute for it the palatal nasal /ɲ/ (see 16.3.3), but the objective reality of its existence in French cannot reasonably be denied.

16.4   The Release of Final Consonants

In English, a final lateral or nasal may not be released, i.e. the speech organs may remain for a while at the point of articulation. For example, in an utterance such as *I'm going home* the lips, which had been closed for the final /m/ of *home*, remain closed, or, at the end of *come down* or *very well*, the tip of the tongue may not be detached immediately from its point of articulation, viz. the alveoli, for the final /n/ or /l/. In French, however, care must be taken to ensure that the final /r/, /l/ or nasal is properly released in words such as (*je*) *pars* /pa:r/, (*elle est*) *belle* /bɛl/, (*elle est*) *bonne* /bɔn/, (*un*) *signe* /siɲ/, (*le*) *parking* /parkiŋ/.

16.5   Voiceless /l/ and /r/

16.5.1   At the end of words such as *people*, *table*, the /l/ in English functions in effect as a vowel and such words therefore have two syllables. In French, however, when words such as *peuple*, *table* and others ending in a stop or /f/ + /l/ occur before a pause, the *l* is not syllabic and *it is voiceless* (it is, in fact, more like the Welsh *ll* of *Llanelli* than the usual voiced French or English /l/, except that it is much more lightly pronounced than Welsh *ll* and that *ll* is pronounced with the tongue to one side of the mouth). Similarly, /r/ is voiceless in the same circumstances.

   This unvoicing of /l/ and /r/ can be indicated by a subscript [॒], e.g. *peuple* [pœpl̥], *table* [tabl̥], *siècle* /sjɛkl̥/, *aveugle* [avœgl̥], *souffle* [sufl̥], *rompre* [rɔ̃:pr̥], *ombre* [ɔ̃:br̥], *être* [ɛtr̥], *perdre* [pɛrdr̥], *âcre* [ɑ:kr̥], *aigre* [ɛgr̥], *offre* [ɔfr̥].

16.5.2 Note that this unvoicing does not apply when the words in question are followed without a pause by another word. There are two such possibilities:

(i) The following word begins with a vowel, in which case the final consonantal cluster, /pl/, /dr/, etc., of the previous word goes with the following syllable and the /l/ or /r/ is voiced, e.g. *le peuple anglais* /lə pœpl ɑ̃glɛ/, *la table où je travaille* /la tabl u ʒ travaj/, *tu vas être heureux* /ty va ɛtr œrø/, *sans perdre un instant* /sɑ̃ pɛrdr œ̃n ɛ̃stɑ̃/.

(ii) The following word begins with a consonant, in which case the final -*e* of the previous word is pronounced (/ə/) (but see also 16.5.3) and therefore, as in (i) above, the cluster composed of a stop or /f/ + /l/ or /r/ comes at the beginning of a syllable and the /l/ or /r/ is voiced, e.g. *le peuple français* /lə pœplə frɑ̃sɛ/, *la table ronde* /la tablə rɔ̃:d/, *au siècle dernier* /o sjɛklə dɛrnje/, *une ombre noire* /yn ɔ̃brə nwa:r/, *il va être là* /il va ɛtrə la/, *sans perdre son temps* /sɑ̃ pɛrdrə sɔ̃ tɑ̃/, *je t'offre ceci* /ʒə t ɔfrə səsi/.

16.5.3 There is a tendency in familiar speech, and one which seems to be on the increase, to drop /l/ and, even more so, /r/ and the following /ə/ in phonetic contexts of the type discussed in 16.5.2 (ii), e.g. *c'est impossib(le) d'y aller* /se t ɛ̃pɔsib di ale/, *il semb(le) que non* /i sɑ̃b kə nɔ̃/, *il va êt(re) là* /i va ɛt la/, *deux kilomèt(res) carrés* /dø kilɔmɛt kare/, *not(re) maison* /nɔt mezɔ̃/, *l'autre jour* /lot ʒu:r/, *quat(re) francs* /kat frɑ̃/, *tu dois connaît(re) mon frère* /ty dwa kɔnɛt mɔ̃ frɛr/, *il va perd(re) son temps* /i va pɛrd sɔ̃ tɑ̃/, *septemb(re) dernier* /sɛptɑb dɛrnje/, *un grand nomb(re) de personnes* /ɛ̃ grɑ̃ nɔ̃b də pɛrsɔn/, *simp(le) comme bonjour* /sɛ̃p kɔm bɔ̃ʒu:r/, *la règ(le) du jeu* /la rɛg dy ʒø/. This also affects words ending in -*vre*, e.g. *pauv(re) type* /pov tip/, *une liv(re) de beurre* /yn liv də bœ:r/. Though widespread, this feature is best avoided by foreigners until they reach the stage where (i) they are speaking at a normal speed, (ii) they are mixing easily with native-speakers of French who currently use it, and (iii) they feel sure they can get away with it without running the risk of having someone correct them. In general, the dropping of the /r/ is considered as more acceptable than the dropping of the /l/, which is more likely to be regarded as sub-standard.

16.6   Voiceless /m/

A voiceless allophone of /m/, which can also be indicated by a subscript [̥] (see 16.5.1), occurs when it follows the voiceless fricative /s/, in words such as *asthme* [asm̥], *spasme* [spasm̥]. This is a type of progressive assimilation (see chapter 18 and especially 18.1.4 and 18.3). Apart from a few relatively infrequent words such as these, it occurs in the ending *-isme* of *communisme* [kɔmynism̥], *nationalisme* [nasjɔnalism̥], *cubisme* [kybism̥], *réalisme* [realism̥], etc. (A pronunciation in /izm/, i.e. with a voiced fricative and, consequently, a voiced /m/ also exists but is less widespread.)

Similarly, a voiceless [m̥] occurs after the voiceless stop /t/ in *rythme* [ritm̥].

17 Gemination

17.1 Long Consonants and Geminate Consonants

17.1.1 We have seen (9.5.3) that consonants that are subject to emphatic stress can be lengthened, and that this lengthening can be indicated in phonetic script by a colon, e.g. "*magnifique* [m:aɲifik].

17.1.2 We have also seen (11.2.4 and 11.6) that, when a mute *e* is dropped, two consonants that would otherwise be separated by /ə/ are brought together, e.g. the /np/ in *je n(e) peux pas* /ʒə n pø pɑ/ or the /fn/ in *la fenêtre* /la fnɛtr/. It frequently happens in such circumstances that the /ə/ that is dropped is both preceded and followed by the same consonant, e.g. *je l(e) lis*, *tu n(e) nages pas*, *cett(e) tasse*. Utterances such as these are represented in phonetic script as if the consonant were in fact doubled, e.g. (to take the examples just given) /ʒə l li/, /tyn naʒ pɑ/, /sɛt tɑːs/. This is justifiable, but explanation is called for:

17.1.3 In an utterance such as *cette porte* /sɛt pɔrt/, the /t/ of *cette* and the /p/ of *porte* are each complete in the sense that they each have the three stages of closing, holding and release (see 14.2.1). This is not so of the /t/ of *cette* and the /t/ of *tasse* in *cette tasse* (for further examples see 17.2.1). What we have here is (i) the closing stage of the first /t/, (ii) a prolonged holding stage, and (iii) the release stage of the second /t/. It could be claimed (but see below) that what we have in such contexts is a 'double' consonant.

It could be and sometimes is argued, however, that what we have in the middle of /sɛt tɑːs/ is neither two consonants, nor a 'double' consonant, but a long consonant. There does however seem to be a valid distinction between the long consonant of *tu* "*mens!* pronounced with emphatic stress, i.e. [ty m:ɑ̃], and the 'double' consonant of *tu m(e) mens* /tym mɑ̃/.

Since neither 'long consonant' nor 'double consonant' is a totally acceptable term, such phonetic features as the /tt/ of *cette tasse* or the /ll/ of *je le lis* are generally referred to as 'geminate' (i.e. 'twin') consonants.

17.1.4 The phenomenon of gemination can easily be illustrated from English minimal pairs such as the following, in which the item in the first column has a simple consonant (as in *eight apes* /eɪt eɪps/) and the one in the second column has a geminate (as in *eight tapes* /eɪt teɪps/):

Simple	Geminate
her book	herb book
white eye	white tie
big earl	big girl
both eyes	both thighs
five ices	five vices
this ink	this sink
free zone	freeze zone
I'm aching	I'm making
ten aims	ten names

Examples involving other consonants are: *black king*, *tough fight*, *full life*.

Geminates in English are sometimes reduced to simple consonants, especially in the middle of compound words, e.g. *bookcase*, *fish-shop*, *unknown*, which may be heard pronounced with either a simple /k/, /ʃ/, /n/ respectively or with a geminate. This must not be imitated in French: except in the special case dealt with in 17.2.5 below, geminates are geminates and must be pronounced as such.

17.2 French Geminates

17.2.1 The majority of French geminates are accounted for by contexts in which a mute *e* is dropped (see 17.1.2). The following are examples of minimal pairs similar to those quoted from English in 17.1.4:

Simple		*Geminate*	
cette aire	/sɛt ɛːr/	*cette terre*	/sɛt tɛːr/
tu trompes	/ty trɔ̃ːp/	*tu te trompes*	/ty t trɔ̃ːp/
la dent	/la dã/	*là-dedans*	/la ddã/
(il) vient dire	/il vjɛ̃ diːr/	*il vient de dire*	/il vjɛ̃ d diːr/
neuf rangs	/nœf rã/	*neuf francs*	/nœf frã/
tu manques	/ty mãːk/	*tu me manques*	/ty m mãːk/
une oie	/yn wa/	*une noix*	/yn nwa/
elle a vu	/ɛl a vy/	*elle l'a vu*	/ɛl la vy/
pour animer	/pur anime/	*pour ranimer*	/pur ranime/

17.2.2 The distinction between a simple and a geminate consonant is particularly significant in the case of verbs whose stem ends in -*r*- and in which forms with a simple consonant represent the imperfect indicative tense while forms with a geminate represent the conditional. There are two classes of such verbs, viz.:

(i) -*er* verbs in which a mute *e* is dropped in the conditional, e.g.:

Imperfect		*Conditional*	
j'adorais	/ʒadɔrɛ/	*j'adorerais*	/ʒadɔrrɛ/
(tu) espérais	/ɛsperɛ/	*(tu) espérerais*	/ɛsperrɛ/
(il) demeurait	/dəmœrɛ/	*(il) demeurerait*	/dəmœrrɛ/
(ils) viraient	/virɛ/	*(ils) vireraient*	/virrɛ/

This situation does not arise in the case of the 1st and 2nd persons plural, e.g. (*nous*) *jurions*, (*vous*) *juriez* /ʒyrjɔ̃/, /ʒyrje/, (*nous*) *jurerions*, (*vous*) *jureriez* /ʒyrərjɔ̃/, /ʒyrərje/

(ii) the verbs *courir* and *mourir*, in which there is no mute *e*, even in writing:

Imperfect	Conditional
(*je*) *courais* /kurɛ/	(*je*) *courrais* /kurrɛ/
(*nous*) *courions* /kurjɔ̃/	(*nous*) *courrions* /kurrjɔ̃/
(*il*) *mourait* /murɛ/	(*il*) *mourrait* /murrɛ/

and in the relatively infrequent verbs *acquérir*, *conquérir*, *s'enquérir* and *requérir*, in which case there is also a difference in the preceding vowel (/e/ ~ /ɛ/):

Imperfect	Conditional
(*il*) *acquérait* /akerɛ/	(*il*) *acquerrait* /akɛrrɛ/

Note that in the future and conditional of the verbs *pouvoir* and *voir* the -*rr*- does not represent a geminate consonant, e.g. (*il*) *pourra* /pura/, (*je*) *verrai* /vɛre/.

17.2.3 A similar distinction also occurs, in the 3rd person singular only, between the past historic and the future of 1st conjugation verbs (i.e. -*er* verbs) whose stem ends in -*r*-, e.g.:

Past historic	Future
(*il*) *adora* /adɔra/	(*il*) *adorera* /adɔrra/

but this is relatively unimportant given the fact that the past historic is virtually never used in everyday spoken French.

17.2.4 Further examples, where there is no question of a minimal pair, are *une robe bleue* /yn rɔb blø/, *netteté* /nɛtte/, *avec qui?* /avɛk ki/, *si je jugeais que* [...] /si ʒ ʒyʒɛ kə/, *au même moment* /o mɛm mɔmã/, *verrerie* /vɛrri/.

17.2.5 Geminates can – and frequently do – occur in the middle of words, in particular:

(i) some words having the negative prefix *il*-, *im*-, *in*- or *ir*-, e.g. *illégal* /illegal/ (see also 13.3.2), *immoral* /immɔral/, *innombrable* /innɔ̃brabl/, *irréel* /irreɛl/, *irrésistible* /irrezistibl/, *irresponsable* /irrɛspɔ̃sabl/

(ii) some words having the prefix *al-*, or *il-*, *im-*, *in-* in a non-negative sense, e.g. *alléger* /alleʒe/, *allocation* /allɔkasjɔ̃/, *illuminer* /illymine/ (see also 13.3.2), *immense* /immɑ̃:s/, *immigrer* /immigre/, *inné* /inne/

(iii) a few other words, including *grammaire* /grammɛ:r/, *satellite* /satɛllit/, *sommaire* /sɔmmɛ:r/, *syllabe* /sillab/.

It is, however, acceptable to pronounce any of the above with a simple consonant, particularly those in (ii) (e.g. *allocation* /alɔkasjɔ̃/, *immense* /imɑ̃s/) and (iii) (e.g. *grammaire* /gramɛ:r/, *satellite* /satelit/), while very many other words having a written double consonant are usually and in many cases always pronounced with a simple consonant: these include (to give only a few examples by way of illustration) *accommoder* /akɔmɔde/, *accompagner* /akɔ̃paɲe/, *accord* /akɔ:r/, *addition* /adisjɔ̃/, *affecter* /afɛkte/, *aggraver* /agrave/, *allumer* /alyme/, *allure* /aly:r/, *apprécier* /apresje/, *arranger* /arɑ̃ʒe/, *arrogant* /arɔgɑ̃/, *attaque* /atak/, *atterrir* /ateri:r/, *commémorer* /kɔmemɔre/, *commencer* /kɔmɑ̃se/, *commission* /kɔmisjɔ̃/, *connaissance* /kɔnɛsɑ̃s/, *correct* /kɔrɛkt/, *correspondant* /kɔrɛspɔ̃dɑ̃/, *innocent* /inɔsɑ̃/, *intelligent* /ɛ̃teliʒɑ̃/, *occuper* /ɔkype/, *sottise* /sɔti:z/.

As it is impossible to give hard and fast rules, the most appropriate advice is probably, in case of uncertainty, to pronounce a simple consonant rather than a geminate: a simple consonant will always be acceptable, even if in some words it is less usual than a geminate, whereas to pronounce a geminate instead of a simple consonant would be unacceptable.

18 Consonantal Assimilation

18.1 Introduction

18.1.1 The point has already been made (1.2.1) that, when we speak, we do not do so in discrete units, i.e. a word such as French /kap/ (written *cap*) does not consist of three unrelated sounds corresponding to the three characters of its printed equivalent. When we speak, the speech organs are not static but, apart from brief intervals of silence, are constantly moving from the position required for one sound to that required for a later sound in the same or a following word. When we are in the process of uttering one sound, the way in which it is pronounced is very likely to be affected by the fact that, at the moment we are uttering it, we are also preparing to utter a later sound. Furthermore, it can also happen – though less frequently – that the precise way in which a given sound is pronounced is influenced by a preceding sound.

18.1.2 If we assume that a given word has three phonemes:

$$1 - 2 - 3$$

and that the pronunciation of '2' is affected by that of '1' and/ or of '3', i.e. that, in some respect or other, the pronunciation of '2' is more like that of '1' and/or '3' than it would otherwise be, we can say that phoneme '2' is, to that extent, **assimilated** to '1' and/or '3'.

18.1.3   The point can be illustrated by taking some simple examples from English:

(i) in a word such as *can* /kæn/, in which a vowel is followed by a nasal consonant, the vowel in question is slightly nasalized, i.e. some air escapes through the nose while the vowel is being pronounced because of the fact that the velum and uvula are beginning to be lowered in preparation for the utterance of the following nasal consonant; to the extent that this happens, the vowel /æ/ is partly assimilated to the /n/

(ii) whereas in *I have no time*, and *has he arrived?*, the final consonants of *have* and *has* are voiced /v/ and /z/ respectively, most people would probably pronounce *I have to* (as in *I have to do it*) and *he has to* with a final voiceless fricative, viz. /f/ and /s/; the reason for this is that, in the expressions in question, the fricative is followed by a voiceless stop /t/ and the vocal cords stop vibrating too soon in preparation for the /t/, with the result that the fricatives themselves become voiceless; the fricatives are therefore assimilated to the /t/ in terms of voicelessness

(iii) in words such as *comfort*, *symphony*, *emphasis*, in which /m/ is followed by /f/, most people utter not – as they may well think – a normal bilabial /m/ but a nasal consonant whose point of articulation is that of the following fricative /f/ – i.e. they are pronouncing a nasal not with closure of the lips, as for a normal /m/, but with the top teeth touching the bottom lip; the nasal is therefore assimilated to the following fricative in terms of its point of articulation; similarly, an /m/ may be substituted for an /n/ before /p/ or /b/ as when *Tenby*, *ten pas(t) five*, *han(d)bag* are pronounced *Temby*, *tem pas(t) five*, *hambag* – the point of articulation, which is normally alveolar, is assimilated to that of the following bilabial stop.

In the above examples, in which a sound is assimilated to a following sound, i.e. in which one sound affects the pronunciation of a preceding one, we have instances of **regressive assimilation**.

18.1.4 Progressive assimilation, in which one sound exercises an assimilatory effect on a following sound, is relatively uncommon in English, but it does occur.

The *s* of *is*, when the word is pronounced in full, is a voiced fricative, /z/, as it is also when reduced to *'s* after a voiced consonant, as in *John's looking for you*. But after a voiceless consonant, as in *What's the matter?*, *it's me*, *Pete's looking for you*, *Cliff's coming*, it is pronounced as /s/, i.e. it becomes voiceless as the result of assimilation to the preceding consonant.

18.1.5   In this chapter, we are concerned with assimilation only in so far as it affects consonants. The phenomenon of 'vowel harmony' (see 10.6.5) is, of course, a type of assimilation affecting vowels.

18.2   Regressive Assimilation of Fortes and Lenes

18.2.1   We saw (6.4.1) that the principal distinction between such pairs as /t/ and /d/, /s/ and /z/, etc., is that /t/ and /s/ are voiceless (i.e. pronounced without vibration of the vocal cords) whereas /d/ and /z/ are voiced, i.e. accompanied by vibration of the vocal cords. We also saw (6.4.2), however, that the resonance and hence the 'carrying power' of a voiced consonant is greater than that of its voiceless equivalent and that this may be compensated for by pronouncing voiceless consonants with greater energy and breath. If we adopt a widely used pair of technical terms, we can say that the 'strong' (i.e. voiceless) consonants are fortis (plural *fortes*) and that the 'weak' (i.e. voiced) consonants are lenis (plural *lenes*).

18.2.2   The most widespread type of assimilation in French is regressive assimilation of voiced consonants, i.e. a voiced consonant becomes voiceless when in contact with a following voiceless consonant. This, however, does not necessarily mean (though it may – see 18.2.4) that the corresponding voiceless fortis (say, /t/ or /ʃ/) is substituted for a voiced lenis (in the cases in point, /d/ and /ʒ/). It is possible that what is uttered in such circumstances is neither a voiceless fortis nor a voiced lenis but a voiceless lenis – i.e. a consonant that is voiceless but has the weak articulation (in terms of expenditure of energy and breath) that is normally characteristic of a voiced consonant. Such sounds can be represented by the symbol for a voiced consonant with a subscript [˳], the usual indication of voicelessness, e.g. /d̥/, /ʒ̥/.

18.2.3   The type of regressive assimilation in question is particularly common in contexts in which /d/ for *de* or /ʒ/ for *je* occurs before a voiceless stop or fricative, e.g.:

(*un*) *coup de pied* [ku d̥ pje]	*je parle* [ʒ̥ parl]
(*un*) *morceau de pain* [mɔrso d̥ pɛ̃]	*je peux* [ʒ̥ pø]
(*un*) *coup de fil* [ku d̥ fil]	*je prends le train* [ʒ̥ prɑ̃ l trɛ̃]
(*le*) *chemin de fer* [ʃmɛ̃ d̥ fɛːr]	*je trouve* [ʒ̥ truːv]
tout de suite [tu d̥ sɥit]	*je te dis* [ʒ̥ tə di]
(*le*) *droit de chasse* [drwa d̥ ʃas]	*je comprends* [ʒ̥ kɔ̃prɑ̃]
(*le*) *rez-de-chaussée* [re d̥ ʃose]	*je fais attention* [ʒ̥ fɛ atɑ̃sjɔ̃]
	je suis là [ʒ̥ sɥi la]
	je savais [ʒ̥ savɛ]

The loss of a mute *e* likewise gives rise to pronunciations such as *médecin* /med̥sɛ̃/, *au-dessous* /od̥su/, *là-dessus* /lad̥sy/.

18.2.4   The type of assimilation referred to in 18.2.3 is very frequently carried further, especially in rapid speech, to the extent that the voiceless lenes /d̥/ and /ʒ̥/ become the normal voiceless fortes /t/ and /ʃ/, e.g.:

tout de suite /tut sɥit/	*je peux* /ʃ pø/
chemin de fer /ʃmɛ̃ t fɛːr/	*je trouve* /ʃ truːv/
médecin /metsɛ̃/	*je te dis* /ʃ tə di/
là-dessus /latsy/	*je suis là* /ʃ sɥi la/

Note that in the middle of words in which *b* precedes /t/ or /s/, the pronunciation with a voiceless fortis, i.e. /p/, is normal, e.g. *obtenir* /ɔptəniːr/, *subtil* /syptil̬/, *absent* /apsɑ̃/, *absolu* /apsɔly/, *abstrait* /apstrɛ/, *absurde* /apsyrd/, *obscur* /ɔpskyːr/, *observer* /ɔpsɛrve/, *obstiné* /ɔpstine/.

18.2.5   Assimilation of a voiceless consonant to a following voiced consonant also occurs, though much less widely than the regressive assimilation of voiced consonants discussed in 18.2.4. This type of assimilation often affects the first consonant only to the extent of producing a voiced fortis, indicated by a subscript [ˌ], e.g. (*la*) *coupe de France* [kup də frɑːs̬], *dites donc!* [dit̬ dɔ̃], *vingt-deux* [vɛ̃t̬dø] (note that *vingt* + a numeral is pronounced /vɛ̃t/ not /vɛ̃/, e.g. *vingt-cinq* /vɛ̃tsɛ̃ːk/), *chaque jour* [ʃak̬ ʒuːr], *avec moi* [avɛk̬ mwa], *deux secondes* [dø s̬gɔ̃ːd] (note that, despite the spelling, *second*, *seconde* are pronounced /səgɔ̃, səgɔ̃ːd/), *une tasse de café* [yn tas̬ də kafe].

Assimilation may, however, be taken to the extent of producing a normal voiced lenis, e.g. *vingt-deux* /vɛ̃ddø/ (with a geminate consonant), *deux secondes* /dø zgɔ̃ːd/. A voiced lenis is usual in the word *anecdote* /anɛgdɔt/, but otherwise this type of assimilation may safely be ignored by foreigners.

18.3   Progressive Assimilation

18.3.1   Progressive assimilation is relatively uncommon in French (as in English, see 18.1.4). It occurs in particular in the following contexts:

18.3.2   A voiceless [m̥] occurs after /s/ as in *asthme* [asm̥], *communisme* [kɔmynism̥], or /t/, *rythme* [ritm̥] (see 16.6).

18.3.3   A voiceless allophone of /v/, viz. /ɣ̊/ (or sometimes the corresponding voiceless phoneme /f/) can occur after /ʃ/, as in *ce cheval* [sə ʃɣ̊al], *les cheveux* [le ʃɣ̊ø].

18.3.4 A type of assimilation that foreigners should be aware of but that they need not imitate is that in which the voiced stops, i.e. bilabial /b/, dental /d/ and velar /g/, are replaced by the corresponding nasal consonants, /m/, /n/ and /ŋ/, by assimilation to a preceding nasal vowel, e.g.:

> *un demi kilo* /ɛ̃ nmi kilo/ for /ɛ̃ (*or* œ̃) dmi kilo/
> *vingt-deux* /vɛ̃ndø/ for /vɛ̃ddø/ (see 18.2.5)
> (*la*) *Chamb*(*re*) *de commerce* /ʃɑ̃m dɛ kɔmɛrs/ for /ʃɑ̃b
> də kɔmɛrs/ (for /ʃɑ̃brə d kɔmɛrs/ – see 11.10)
> (*une*) *longue main* /lɔ̃ŋ mɛ̃/ for /lɔ̃g mɛ̃/
> (*les*) *langues modernes* /lɑ̃ŋ mɔdɛrn/ for /lɑ̃g mɔdɛrn/

18.3.5 A voiceless allophone of the semi-consonants /j/, /ɥ/, /w/, is regularly used after a voiceless consonant, e.g. *pied* [pje], *tiens* [tjɛ̃], *fier* [fjɛːr], *puis* [pɥi], *cuisine* [kɥizin], *tueur* [tɥœːr], *poire* [pw̥aːr], *toi* [tw̥a].

18.4 Assimilation to Vowels

We have seen (10.1.1) that lip movements are much more vigorous and (because of the greater degree of tension involved) more sharply defined in French than in English. Related to this is the fact that the articulation of French consonants is very much influenced by the lip position adopted for the vowel that they precede or follow in the same syllable.

We can discuss this first in relation to consonants at the beginning of a syllable. In English, many native-speakers anticipate the vowel of words such as, on the one hand, *too*, *cool*, *loop*, by rounding the lips to some extent, or, on the other, the vowel of words such as *tea*, *keel*, *leap*, by spreading the lips to some extent. (Southern English speakers are less likely to do so than others, and consequently more likely to pronounce *too*, *cool*, etc., as something like [təu], [kəul] – see 10.4.) In French, this anticipation of the vowel is much more marked than in any variety of English: the lips are markedly rounded for the pronunciation of words such as *tout* /tu/, *cour* /ku:r/, and markedly spread for the pronunciation of words such as *tige* /ti:ʒ/, *qui* /ki/, and these lip-positions, and others that are appropriate for other vowels (e.g. /e/ in *thé* /te/, /ɛ/ in *telle* /tɛl/, /ø/ in *queue* /kø/, or /œ/ in *sœur* /sœ:r/), are very positively taken up *before* the initial consonant is uttered. This can also affect consonant clusters such as /tr/ – the cluster is pronounced with spread lips in *tri* /tri/, but with rounded lips in *trou* /tru/.

This feature of French pronunciation is often referred to as 'vowel anticipation', a term that is not inaccurate as far as it goes. It does not, however, go far enough, since this assimilation to the vowel in respect of lip-position also affects consonants that follow a vowel in the same syllable. For example, the /t/ of *vite* /vit/, the /k/ of *tic* /tik/, the /s/ of *vis* /vis/, the /l/ of *vile* /vil/, the /tr/ of *litre* /litr/ and the /vr/ of *livre* /li:vr/ are pronounced with spread lips, and the corresponding final consonants or clusters of *voûte* /vut/, *souk* /suk/, *tous* /tus/, *foule* /ful/, *l'outre* /lutr/, *Louvre* /lu:vr/ with rounded lips.

19 Liaison

19.1 Origins

19.1.1 The fact that so many French words end in a written but, in most contexts, unpronounced consonant (e.g. *trop* /tro/, *champ* /ʃɑ̃/, *sujet* /syʒɛ/, *cent* /sɑ̃/, *blanc* /blɑ̃/, *murs* /my:r/, (*vous*) *avez* /ave/, *gentil* /ʒɑ̃ti/, *chanter* /ʃɑ̃te/) has its origins as far back as the end of the twelfth century. At that time, final consonants began to disappear before another word beginning with a consonant (e.g., to quote a few cases in their modern form, the -*p* of *trop* in *trop tôt*, the -*t* of *huit* in *huit jours*, the -*s* of *gros* in *un gros livre*). By the end of the Old French period, i.e. by about the year 1300 or a little later, they had probably completely disappeared in this position. But before a vowel and before a pause they remained. Consequently, very many words had two different pronunciations, as is still the case with the numerals *cinq* and *huit* which lose their final consonant before a consonant (*cinq francs* /sɛ̃ frɑ̃/, *huit jours* /ɥi ʒu:r/), but keep it before a vowel (*cinq enfants* /sɛk ɑ̃fɑ/, *huit heures* /ɥit œ:r/) or before a pause (*j'en ai cinq* /ʒɑ̃ e sɛ̃:k/, *jusqu'à huit* /ʒyska ɥit/).

In the Middle French period, therefore, i.e. during the fourteenth and fifteenth centuries, and probably later, many words ending in a consonant followed this pattern. Consequently, words like *drap*, *lit*, *sac*, *vif*, *os*, and hundreds of others with them had alternative forms, /dra/ ~ /drap/, /li/

~ /lit/, /sa/ ~ /sak/, etc., the first being used before a consonant, the second before a vowel or before a pause.

The situation was even more complicated in the case of words ending in /f/ or /s/, since these consonants not only disappeared before a consonant and remained before a pause but voiced to /v/ and /z/ respectively before a vowel. Consequently, words like *vif, os*, had the three pronunciations /vi/ ~ /vif/ ~ /viv/, /o/ ~ /ɔs/ ~ /ɔz/. This state of affairs remains in the case of the numerals *six* and *dix* (which used to be written *sis, dis*), e.g. *j'en ai six* /ʒɑ̃n e sis/, *jusqu'à dix* /ʒyska dis/ ~ *six livres* /si liːvr/, *dix jours* /di ʒuːr/ ~ *six ans* /siz ɑ̃/, *dix heures* /diz œːr/.

In later centuries, the situation was considerably simplified.

19.1.2 In many words, one single form survives in all positions, i.e. before a consonant, before a vowel, or before a pause. This may be either the form with a pronounced consonant (e.g. *cap* /kap/, *sac* /sak/, *vif* /vif/, *sens* /sɑ̃ːs/, *péril* /peril/, *amer* /amɛːr/, *finir* /finiːr/, *avoir* /avwaːr/) or, more frequently, the form without a pronounced consonant (e.g. *champ* /ʃɑ̃/, *dent* /dɑ̃/, *flot* /flo/, *broc* /bro/, *clef* /kle/, *dos* /do/, *fusil* /fyzi/, (*le*) *boucher* /buʃe/, *chanter* /ʃɑ̃te/).

19.1.3 Elsewhere, the form without a consonant remains before a consonant or before a pause, while a form with a pronounced final consonant has been retained in some or all contexts when the word is followed without a pause by a vowel, e.g. *il est petit* /il ɛ pti/ ~ *le petit enfant* /lə ptit ɑ̃fɑ̃/, *moins grand* /mwɛ̃ grɑ̃/ ~ *moins utile* /mwɛz ytil/, *les murs gris* /le myr gri/ ~ *les murs épais* /le myrz epɛ/. (One can compare the use of forms with and without a pronounced /r/ in Standard British English, e.g. [without /r/] *four days, for me, where did you go?*, [with /r/] *four apples, for everybody, where are you going?*)

These special forms for use before vowels are known as **liaison** forms and the purpose of this chapter is to examine in which circumstances they are or are not used.

19.2   The Problem

19.2.1   If all we had to do was to lay down a set of rules determining (i) when a liaison is made and (ii) when it is not, this would probably be straightforward. Unfortunately, things are not that simple. We can certainly define conditions in which a liaison *must* be made and others in which it must not, but in between there is a grey area, which, moreover, is not of a uniform shade of grey: conditions range from those in which liaison is usual except in very familiar speech via those in which it is more or less optional to those in which it is not normal but may occur in very formal and perhaps slightly archaic discourse.

19.2.2   To simplify the matter as far as possible without distorting linguistic realities, we shall consider three categories, viz. (i) those in which liaison is compulsory (19.5), (ii) those in which liaison is usual except sometimes in familiar speech (19.6), and (iii) those in which an uninformed foreigner may well assume that liaison occurs, but where, in reality, it is either not normal in conversation or totally impossible (19.7). The reader is reminded, however, that what follows does represent something of a simplification. An even more simplified approach (and one that would not lead one seriously astray) that could be adopted, at least until the learner has spent a fair amount of time in a French-speaking environment and can form his or her own judgement, would be to use the liaison form consistently in the contexts covered in 19.6.

19.2.3   The indications given below ought to ensure that an acceptable solution to the problem is arrived at in the vast majority of cases, but the situation *is* extremely complicated and it is quite impossible, in the space of a few pages, to cover all eventualities. This is illustrated by the fact that Pierre Fouché's *Traité de prononciation française* (1969) devotes forty-six pages (434–79) to the subject, and even this does not claim to be an exhaustive treatment. The reader is referred to the chapter in question (on which the following – and in particular sections 19.6 and 19.7 – is to some extent based) for further details. It should be noted, however, that the basis of Fouché's analysis is not familiar speech but careful speech or reading aloud for everyday purposes, though indications both as to more familiar and as to more formal styles are given.

The overriding consideration is that liaison can occur only within a rhythmic group and even then, generally speaking, only if there is some close grammatical or semantic link between the two words concerned.

19.3   The Liaison Forms

19.3.1   Before embarking on our summary survey of the contents in which liaison does or does not occur, we must first specify what the liaison forms – i.e. the forms that words take in contexts requiring or allowing liaison – in fact are.

Liaison forms can be categorized in a variety of ways. The one adopted here is perhaps the simplest. It must be recognized, however, that a purist could certainly object, and not without reason, that a description that rests on the assumption that, in French, a given written character normally (though not of course by any means invariably) corresponds in some way or other to a given phoneme (e.g. *t* to /t/) is not entirely defensible.

19.3.2   The liaison form frequently corresponds to the written form in the sense that a written form that is otherwise not pronounced *is* pronounced, and with its 'normal' value, in the liaison form.

If we leave out of account words ending in a nasal (see 19.3.6) and a very few other relatively uncommon words or expressions, we can say that this category is in effect limited to:

(i) words ending in -*t*, e.g. *petit* /pəti/ but *un petit enfant* /œ̃ ptit ɑ̃fɑ̃/, *tout* /tu/ but *tout à fait* /tut a fɛ/, *il est là* /il ɛ la/

but *il est ici* /il ɛt isi/, *tant* /tã/ but *je l'ai tant aimé* /ʒə le tãt eme/, *haut* /o/ but *de haut en bas* /də ot ã bɑ/, *vingt livres* /vɛ̃ liːvr/ but *vingt élèves* /vɛ̃t elɛːv/, *il dit* /il di/ but *que dit-il?* /kə dit il/

(ii) the preposition *chez* /ʃe/ and verb forms ending in *-ez*, e.g. *chez eux* /ʃez ø/, *vous avez fini* /vuz ave fini/ but *vous avez entendu* /vuz avez ãtãdy/

(iii) the words *beaucoup* /boku/ and *trop* /tro/, e.g. *je l'ai beaucoup aimé* /ʒe le bokup eme/, *il a trop hésité* /il a trop ezite/, *trop à faire* /trop a fɛːr/, *trop ennuyeux* /trop ãnɥijø/; *trop* has the minor complication that, in the liaison form, the vowel may be opened to /ɔ/, e.g. /trɔp ezite/, /trɔp a fɛːr/, but in ordinary conversational usage /trop/ is more usual and that is the form that will be adopted below in the phonetic representation of examples involving *trop*

(iv) the adjectives *premier* /prəmje/, *dernier* /dɛrnje/ and *léger* /leʒe/; note that in the liaison form the vowel /e/ is frequently opened to /ɛ/, particularly in careful speech (in which case the words in question are therefore pronounced like the feminine forms *première, dernière, légère*), e.g. *le premier homme* /lə prəmjer ɔm/ or /lɛ prəmjɛr ɔm/, *le dernier arrêt* /lə dɛrnjer arɛ/ or /lə dɛrnjɛr arɛ/, *un léger espoir* /œ̃ leʒer ɛspwaːr/ or /œ̃ leʒɛr ɛspwaːr/.

19.3.3   The liaison form of words ending in *-s* or in *-x* ends in /z/, e.g. *dans un livre* /dãz œ̃ liːvr/, *sous un arbre* /suz œ̃n arbr/, *pas encore* /pɑz ãkɔːr/, *plus ou moins* /plyz u mwɛ̃/, *nous avons été* /nuz avɔ̃z ete/, *les innocents* /lez inɔsã/, *mes bons amis* /me bɔ̃z ami/, *les grands arbres* /le grãz arbr/, *quels enfants?* /kɛlz ãfã/, *un malheureux accident* /œ̃ malhœrøz aksidã/, *deux enfants* /døz ãfã/, *six ans* /siz ã/, *dix heures* /diz œːr/, *tes beaux yeux* /te boz jø/.

As many of the above examples show, this type of liaison form frequently occurs with plurals and is therefore particularly widespread.

19.3.4 The words *quand*, *grand*, *second* and 3rd person singular verb forms in *-d* have a liaison form in /t/, e.g. *quand il viendra* /kɑ̃t il vjɛ̃dra/, *un grand homme* /œ̃ grɑ̃t ɔm/, *un second enfant* /œ̃ sgɔ̃t ɑ̃fɑ̃/, *que prend-il?* /kə prɑ̃t il/, *qu'attend-on?* /katɑ̃t ɔ̃/.

(The reason for this is that, in medieval French, these words were pronounced with a /t/ and written with a *t*, i.e. *quant*, *grant*, (*il*) *prent*, etc. The spelling has since been modified under the influence of the corresponding Latin words, *quando*, *grandis*, *secundus*, or, in the case of the verbs, on the basis of the infinitive, *prendre*, *attendre*, and, in some instances, other persons of the verb such as *nous attendons*, *ils attendent*.)

19.3.5 The word *neuf* /nœf/ 'nine' has the liaison form /nœv/ in the two phrases *neuf heures* /nœv œ:r/ and *neuf ans* /nœv ɑ̃/ only.

19.3.6 In the case of the liaison form of words ending in a nasal vowel in pronunciation and an *n* in spelling, there are two possibilities:

(i) The nasal vowel remains unchanged and the *n* appears as a liaison consonant. This occurs in particular with the pronouns *on* /ɔ̃/ and *en* /ɑ̃/, e.g. *on arrive* /ɔ̃n ari:v/, *il en a beaucoup* /il ɑ̃n a boku/, with the determiners *un* /œ̃/ or /ɛ̃/ (see 10.10.3) and *aucun* /okœ̃/ or /okɛ̃/, e.g. *un accident* /œ̃n aksidɑ̃/ or /ɛ̃n aksidɑ̃/, *aucun ennemi* /okœ̃n ɛnmi/ or /œkɛ̃n ɛnmi/, with the preposition *en*, e.g. *en Allemagne* /ɑ̃n almaɲ/, and with *bien* and *rien*, e.g. *bien aimable* /bjɛ̃n ɛmabl/, *rien à declarer* /rjɛ̃n a deklare/.

(ii) In *bon* and in masculine singular adjectives ending in *-ain*, *-ein*, *-ien* or *-yen*, the vowel is denasalized and the *n* is pronounced, with the result that the pronunciation is identical to that of the corresponding feminine adjective. The adjectives principally affected, in addition to *bon* /bɔ̃/, e.g. *un bon élève* /œ̃ bɔn elɛ:v/, are *certain*, particularly in the expression *d'un certain âge* /dœ̃ sɛrtɛn ɑ:ʒ/, *plein* /plɛ̃/, particularly in such expressions as *le* (or *en*) *plein air* /lə (ᾱ) plɛn ɛːr/, *en plein été* /ᾱ plɛn ete/, *le plein-emploi* /lə plɛnᾱplwa/, *ancien* /ᾱsjɛ̃/, e.g. *un ancien élève* /œ̃n ᾱsjɛn elɛːv/, and *moyen*, especially in (*le*) *moyen-âge* /mwajɛnɑːʒ/ and *Moyen Orient* /mwajɛn ɔrjᾱ̃/. (Some educated speakers of French pronounce at least some of these words as if they fell into category (i) above, e.g. *d'un certain âge* /dœ̃ sɛrtɛn ɑːʒ/, but in the case of others, e.g. *plein-emploi*, *moyen-âge*, the pronunciation /ɛn/ seems to be virtually universal. The foreigner is therefore advised to follow the above rule in all cases.)

Note that the possessives *mon*, *ton*, *son* sometimes fall into this category, e.g. *mon esprit* /mɔn ɛspri/, *ton ami* /tɔn ami/, but the pronunciation with a nasal vowel, as in (i) above, is now the usual one, e.g. *mon esprit* /mɔ̃n ɛspri/, *ton ami* /tɔ̃n ami/, and should be adopted by foreigners.

19.3.7 Nine other words (in addition to some verb forms – see 19.3.8) have special written as well as spoken liaison forms:

(i) the masculine singular demonstrative *ce* /sə/: liaison form *cet* /sɛt/, e.g. *ce livre* but *cet arbre* /sɛt arbr/

(ii) the feminine singular possessives *ma*, *ta*, *sa* /ma, ta, sa/: liaison forms *mon*, *ton*, *son* /mɔ̃n, tɔ̃n, sɔ̃n/ (or /mɔn, tɔn, sɔn/ – cf. the end of paragraph 19.3.6), e.g. *ma première étude*, *ta meilleure amie*, *sa maison* but *mon étude* /mɔ̃n etyd/, *ton amie* /tɔ̃n ami/, *son ancienne maison* /sɔ̃n ᾱsjɛn mɛzɔ̃/

(iii) the masculine singular adjectives *beau* /bo/, *nouveau* /nuvo/, *fou* /fu/, *mou* /mu/, *vieux* /vjø/: liaison forms *bel* /bɛl/, *nouvel* /nuvɛl/, *fol* /fɔl/, *mol* /mɔl/, *vieil* /vjɛj/, e.g. *un bel homme* /œ̃ bɛl ɔm/, *le Nouvel An* /lə nuvɛl ᾱ/, *un fol espoir* /œ̃ fɔl ɛspwaːr/, *un mol oreiller* /œ̃ mɔl ɔreje/, *son vieil ennemi* /sɔ̃ vjɛj ɛnmi/.

19.3.8 Third person singular verbs ending in -*e* or in -*a* have a special liaison form in /t/, indicated in writing by -*t*-, when one of the pronoun subjects *il*, *elle*, *on* follows, either in questions or when the normal subject–verb order is inverted for any other reason. This affects principally the present indicative of -er verbs and verbs such as *souffrir*, etc., e.g. *quand arrive-t-il?* /kɑ̃ ariv t il/, *peut-être souffre-t-elle* /pøt ɛtrə sufrə t ɛl/, the singular of the verbs *avoir* (e.g. *'Non', a-t-il répondu* /nɔ̃ a t il repɔ̃dy/ and *aller* (*Où va-t-on?* /u va t ɔ̃/), and the future of all verbs, e.g. *Que dira-t-elle?* /kə dira t ɛl/, *Peut-être viendra-t-il* /pøtɛtrə vjɛ̃ndra t il/. (It also affects the past historic of -er verbs, in so far as these occur in speech, e.g. *Que chanta-t-il?* /kə ʃɑ̃ta t il/.)

19.4 Words Having No Special Liaison Form

19.4.1 The vast majority of words, other than the plurals of nouns and adjectives, have no special liaison forms. Note in particular that the following, for which foreigners are often tempted to invent liaison forms, have no such forms:

19.4.2 The prepositions *vers*, *envers*, *avant* and *selon*, e.g. *vers elle* /vɛr ɛl/, *vers une heure* /vɛr yn œ:r/, *vers Amiens* /vɛr amjɛ̃/, *envers eux* /ɑ̃vɛr ø/, *avant elle* /avɑ̃ ɛl/, *avant une heure* /avɑ̃ yn œ:r/ (note however the adverb *avant-hier* /avɑ̃tjɛ:r/ 'the day before yesterday'), *selon eux* /səlɔ̃ ø/, *selon un membre du groupe* /səlɔ̃ œ̃ mɑ̃brə dy grup/.

19.4.3 Adjectives ending in -*rd* or -*rt*, namely *lourd*, *court* and *fort*, e.g. *un lourd objet* /œ̃ lur ɔbʒɛ/, *un court intervalle* /œ̃ kur ɛ̃tɛrval/, *un fort argument* /œ̃ fɔr argymɑ̃/, but note that when used adverbially, i.e. when meaning 'very', *fort* can have a liaison form, e.g. *fort utile* /fɔrt ytil/ (or, especially in conversational usage, /fɔr ytil/).

19.4.4 Words ending in a written nasal consonant other than those discussed in 19.3.6, e.g. *maison à louer* /mɛzɔ̃ a lwe/, *un million et demi* /œ̃ miljɔ̃ e dmi/.

19.4.5 The conjunction *et*, e.g. *nécessaire et utile* /nesɛsɛ:r e ytil/, *mon collègue et ami* /mɔ̃ kɔlɛg e ami/, *et il s'en va* /e il sɑ̃ va/. (The reason why the -*t* of *et* is *never* pronounced is that the Old French form was *e* – the -*t* was later introduced under the influence of Latin *et*.)

19.5   Compulsory Liaison

19.5.1   Liaison is compulsory, even in conversational usage, in the following contexts:

19.5.2   Within a **noun group**, which for our present purposes is defined as follows:

determiner (+ adjective) + noun

Notes: (i) The determiners that have liaison forms are: in the singular, *un*, *aucun*, *mon*, *ton*, *son*, *cet*; in the plural, *les*, *aux*, *des*, *mes*, *tes*, *ses*, *ces*, *quels*, *quelles*, *certains*, *certaines* 'some, certain', *différents*, *différentes* 'various', *divers*, *diverses* 'various', *plusieurs* and *quelques*; and the numerals *deux*, *trois*, *cinq*, *six*, *huit*, *dix*, *vingt*, *quatre-vingts*, *cent*, *cents* and compounds thereof (e.g. *dix-huit*, *vingt-trois*) (for *neuf*, see 19.3.5).

(ii) (+ adjective) indicates that the group may or may not include an adjective before the noun.

(iii) The term 'noun group' as used here is *not* the equivalent of the widely used term 'noun phrase': note in particular that the noun group as defined here does not include adjectives that come after the noun. ('Noun phrase' would have been from a number of points of view a preferable term but, given that it has now been so firmly pre-empted in another sense, it would be misleading if we were to use it in the sense of 'noun group' as defined above.)

Examples: *un arbre* /œ̃n arbr/, *aucun Anglais* /okœ̃n ãglɛ/, *mon ami* /mɔ̃n ami/, *les Américains* /lez amerikɛ̃/, *aux enfants* /oz ãfã/, *mes amis* /mez ami/, *quels étudiants?* /kɛlz etydjã/, *trois oranges* /trwaz ɔrã:ʒ/, *six élèves* /siz elɛ:v/, *vingt ans* /vɛ̃t ã/, *quatre-vingts ans* /katrəvɛ̃z ã/, *cent ans* /sɑ̃t ɑ̃/, *mon grand ami* /mɔ̃ grɑ̃t ami/, *mon vieil ami* /mɔ̃ vjɛj ami/, *les beaux arbres* /le boz arbr/.

19.5.3   Within a **verb group**, which for our present purposes is defined as follows:

(subject pronoun) + verb + (object pronoun(s))

Notes: (i) The relevant pronouns that may *precede* the verb and which have liaison forms are *on*, *nous*, *vous*, *ils*, *elles* and *les*.

(ii) The relevant pronouns that may *follow* the verb and before which a verb or another pronoun (see (iii) below) has a liaison form are *il*, *elle*, *on*, *ils*, *elles* or (with verbs in the imperative only) *y*, *en*.

(iii) As should be clear from the above comments, the term 'verb group' as used here includes only the verb itself and the subject and object pronouns that are attached to it proclitically (i.e. before the verb) or enclitically (i.e. after the verb); note too that, in the case of compound verbs, only the auxiliary verb is taken into account – i.e. though there *may* be a liaison between the auxiliary and the past participle (e.g. *ils ont été* /ilz ɔ̃t ete/, *je suis allé* /ʒə sɥiz ale/), this is not necessarily the case in all contexts (see 19.6.3).

Within the group, liaison occurs:

(i) between pronoun and verb, e.g. *nous envoyons* /nuz ɑ̃wajɔ̃/, *vous aimez* /vuz eme/, *ils ouvrent* /ilz u:vr/, *elles apportent* /ɛlz apɔrt/, *il nous envoie (un cadeau)* /il nuz ɑ̃vwa/, *je vous aime* /ʒə vuz ɛm/, *il les a vus* /il lez a vy/

(ii) between the verb and a following pronoun subject, e.g. *que fait-on?* /kə fɛt ɔ̃/, *dort-elle?* /dɔrt ɛl/, *a-t-il fini?* /a t il fini/, *que disent-ils?* /kə dizt il/, *chantent-elles?* /ʃɑ̃tət ɛl/

(iii) between a verb in the imperative and a following *y* or *en*, e.g. *allez-y* /alez i/, *apportes-en deux* /apɔrtəz ɑ̃ dø/, *achetons-en* /aʃtɔ̃z ɑ̃/

(iv) between two pronouns, i.e., more specifically, between *nous*, *vous*, *on* or *les* and *y* or *en*, either before the verb, e.g. *il nous en donne* /il nuz ɑ̃ dɔn/, *je les y vois* /ʒə lez i vwa/, or

after an imperative, e.g. *allez-vous-en* /ale vuz ɑ̃/, *laisse-les-y*
/lɛs lez i/.

19.5.4   In a variety of more specific contexts, of which the
following are among those that occur most frequently:
  (i) *dont* + *il(s)*, *elle(s)*, *on*, e.g. (*le sujet*) *dont on parlait*
/dɔ̃t ɔ̃ parlɛ/
  (ii) *tout* 'every' + noun (or + *autre* + noun), e.g. *tout*
écrivain /tut ekrivɛ̃/, *en tout état de cause* /ɑ̃ tut eta d koːz/, *à*
tout instant /a tut ɛ̃stɑ̃/, *tout autre étudiant* /tut otr etydjɑ̃/,
and *tout un* 'a whole', e.g. *tout un livre* /tut œ̃ liːvr/
  tout 'everything' + *est*, *était*, e.g. *tout est possible* /tut ɛ
pɔsibl/ or + participle or infinitive, e.g. *j'ai tout entendu* /ʒe
tut ɑ̃tɑ̃dy/, *il va tout abîmer* /il va tut abime/
  tout 'completely' + adjective, past participle, adverb, or
adverbial expression, e.g. *tout heureux* /tut œrø/, *tout étonné*
/tut etɔne/, *tout autrement* /tut otrəmɑ̃/, *tout aussi bien* /tut
osi bjɛ̃/, *tout en noir* /tut ɑ̃ nwaːr/, *tout à fait* /tut a fɛ/
  (iii) *très*, *bien*, *fort* (see 19.4.3), *plus*, *moins*, *trop* +
adjective, past participle or adverb, e.g. *très aimable* /trɛz
ɛmabl/, *bien utile* /bjɛ̃ ytil/, *on s'est bien amusé* /ɔ̃ sɛ bjɛ̃
amyze/, *fort intéressant* /fɔrt ɛ̃terɛsɑ̃/, *moins avancé* /mwɛz
avɑ̃se/, *plus utilement* /plyz ytilmɑ̃/, *trop heureux* /trop
œrø/
  (iv) *est* or *sont* + the indefinite article (*un*, *une*), an
adjective, a past participle, or an adverb or prepositional
phrase closely linked in meaning with the verb, e.g. *c'est un*
Français /sɛt œ̃ frɑ̃sɛ/, *c'est impossible* /sɛt ɛ̃pɔsibl/, *il est*
heureux /il ɛt œrø/, *elle est arrivée* /ɛl ɛt arive/, *il est ici* /il ɛt
isi/, *ils sont à Paris* /il sɔ̃t a pari/
  (v) *rien* + past participle or before *à* + infinitive, e.g. *je n'ai*
rien acheté /ʒə ne rjɛ̃ aʃte/, *je n'ai rien à déclarer* /ʒə ne rjɛ̃ a
deklare/, *il n'y a rien à faire* /il ni a rjɛ̃ a fɛːr/, but not
elsewhere (e.g. *on ne voit rien ici* /ɔ̃ n vwa rjɛ̃ isi/, *je ne*
comprends rien à cette affaire /ʒə n kɔ̃prɑ̃ rjɛ̃ a sɛt afɛːr/
  (vi) monosyllabic preposition + following word, e.g. *dans*
une boîte /dɑ̃z yn bwat/, *dès à présent* /dɛz a prezɑ̃/, *en Italie*

/ãn itali/, *en attendant* /ã atãdã/, *sans hésiter* /sãz ezite/, *sans avoir lu* /sãz avwar ly/, *chez elle* /ʃez ɛl/, *sous une chaise* /suz yn ʃɛːz/; however, liaison after *chez* is not obligatory before personal names, e.g. *chez Anne* /ʃe an/, *chez Henri* /ʃe ãri/. Note that *vers* has no liaison form (i.e. the -*s* is never pronounced, e.g. *vers eux* /vɛr ø/). For bisyllabic prepositions see 19.6.6.

   (vii) *quand* + *il*(*s*), *elle*(*s*), *on*, e.g. *quand il est parti* /kãt il ɛ parti/, *quand elle arrivera* /kãt ɛl arivra/. (On *quand* introducing a question, see 19.7.9.)

   (viii) in a number of fixed expressions, of the type *de plus en plus* /də plyz ã ply/, *de temps en temps* /də tãz ã tã/, *d'un bout à l'autre* /dœ̃ but a lotr/, *petit à petit* /pətit a pti/.

19.6   Generally Acceptable Liaison

19.6.1 The expression 'generally acceptable liaison' is deliberately vague, in the sense that we are not attempting to define with any great degree of precision what is acceptable and when. Broadly speaking, the contexts covered in this section are those in which the foreigner is unlikely to attract attention either by making a liaison or by failing to make one. In some such contexts, many native-speakers would probably not make a liaison in certain situations whereas they would in others. The degree of formality of the situation is an important factor, with a much greater tendency to make liaisons being noticeable in registers other than familiar conversation. But even in conversation, there may be considerable variation within the speech of one and the same speaker. A person who, in chatting in highly informal situations, e.g. with members of the family or close friends, will restrict use of liaison more or less to the type of contexts discussed in 19.5, *may* (but this is not true of everyone) make wider, and perhaps considerably wider, use of liaison forms when conversing with, say, older people or strangers. Or one may use more such forms, even in casual conversation, on sad or solemn occasions than on light-hearted occasions.

19.6.2 The following, then (19.6.3–19.6.6), are some of the most important contexts in which the use of a liaison form is 'generally acceptable'. One can go even further and advise the foreign learner to use the liaison form in such contexts unless and until his or her own observation of the conversational practice of native-speakers of French suggests that it would be more usual not to do so – and, while we do not wish to complicate the issue unduly here by commenting on every one of the following sub-categories, it will be noticed that, in some but not all contexts, it *is* more usual not to use the liaison form.

19.6.3 Between parts of *être* or *avoir* and a past participle (see also 19.5.4 (iv)) and between parts of *aller* or *devoir* and an infinitive, e.g. *je suis allé* /ʒə sɥiz ale/, *nous sommes arrivés* /nu sɔmz arive/, *tu étais allé* /ty etez ale/, *nous avons écrit* /nuz avɔ̃z ekri/, *vous avez eu* /vuz avez y/, *j'avais été* /ʒavɛz ete/, *ils avaient entendu* /ilz avɛt ɑ̃tɑ̃dy/, *nous allons arriver* /nuz alɔ̃z arive/, *je dois avouer* /ʒə dwaz avwe/. (According to Fouché, 1969: 474, there is, however, no liaison after *tu seras*, *tu as* and *tu auras*.)

19.6.4 Between parts of *être* and a following adjective or noun, e.g. *je suis heureux* /ʒə sɥiz œrø/, *tu es impardonnable* /ty ɛz ɛ̃pardɔnabl/, *vous étiez avocat* /vuz etjez avɔka/.

19.6.5 Between *pas*, *jamais* or *assez* and a following word or phrase with which it is closely associated in meaning, e.g. (*je ne suis*) *pas heureux* /paz œrø/, (*il n'est*) *pas ici* /paz isi/, *pas encore* /paz ɑ̃kɔ:r/, (*ils n'iront*) *pas à Paris* /paz a pari/, (*il n'y a*) *jamais été* /ʒamɛz ete/, (*il n'en a*) *jamais assez* /ʒamɛz ase/, *assez important* /asez ɛ̃pɔrtɑ̃/.

19.6.6 After the bisyllabic prepositions *après*, *depuis*, *devant*, *pendant*, e.g. *après un mois* /aprɛz œ̃ mwa/, *après avoir fini* /aprɛz avwar fini/, *depuis octobre* /dəpɥiz ɔktɔbr/, *devant une fenêtre* /dəvɑ̃t yn fənɛtr/, *pendant une heure* /pɑ̃dɑ̃t yn œ:r/; but note (i) in conversational usage this liaison is frequently not made, (ii) there is no liaison in *après eux* /aprɛ ø/ (but *après elle(s)* /aprɛz ɛl/). (On *envers, avant, selon*, see 19.4.2.)

19.7   No Liaison

19.7.1   Liaison must be avoided in conversational usage (and in some cases does not occur even in a highly formal style) in such contexts as the following:

19.7.2   Between a noun and a following adjective, e.g. (*le*) *gouvernement espagnol* /guvɛrnəmã ɛspaɲɔl/, (*un*) *objet intéressant* /ɔbʒɛ ẽterɛsã/, (*un*) *repas excellent* /rəpɑ ɛksɛlã/, (*un*) *palais imposant* /palɛ ẽpozã/, (*un*) *cas exceptionnel* /kɑ ɛksɛpsjɔnɛl/, (*un*) *coup affreux* /ku afrø/, (*des*) *amis américains* /ami amerikẽ/, (*des*) *enfants intelligents* /ãfã ẽtɛliʒã/, (*des*) *livres intéressants* /livr ẽterɛsã/, (*des*) *objets utiles* /ɔbʒɛ ytil/, (*des*) *personnes opiniâtres* /pɛrsɔn ɔpinja:tr/, (*des*) *châteaux imposants* /ʃato ẽpozã/.

Note however that, *in the plural only*, the liaison forms are sometimes used in a formal style of delivery and are compulsory in a few set expressions such as (*les*) *États-Unis* /etaz yni/ and (*les*) *Nations Unies* /nasjõz yni/. In the singular, the liaison form should never be used except in a very few fixed expressions, the most common of which is *accent aigu* /aksãt egy/.

19.7.3   Between a noun subject and its verb, e.g. *ce cas est difficile* /sə kɑ ɛ difisil/, *le gouvernement a décidé* /lə guvɛrnəmã a deside/, *l'étudiant achète* (*un livre*) /letydjã aʃɛt/, *les enfants étaient là* /lez ãfã etɛ la/, *mes parents ont* (*une belle maison*) /me parã õ/, *nos amis arrivent* /nɔz ami ari:v/, *les oiseaux apparaissent* /lez wazo aparɛs/.

This also applies when the verb group (as defined in 19.5.3) begins with *y* or *en*, e.g. *l'étudiant en trouve* /letydjã ã tru:v/, *nos voisins y travaillent* /no vwazẽ i travaj/.

19.7.4 Between a verb (other than *avoir* or *être*) and any following element including:

   (i) an adjective, e.g. *il devient énorme* /il dəvjɛ̃ enɔrm/, *vous paraissez heureux* /vu parɛse œrø/

   (ii) an infinitive, e.g. *je vais acheter* /ʒə vɛ aʃte/, *il veut écrire* /il vø ekri:r/, *ils voulaient avoir* /il vulɛ avwa:r/

   (iii) a direct object, e.g. *je vois un train* /ʒə vwa œ̃ trɛ̃/, *il a écrit une longue lettre* /il a ekri yn lɔ̃g lɛtr/

   (iv) an adverb or prepositional phrase, e.g. *je pars immédiatement* /ʒə par imedjatmɑ̃/, *vous parlez avec difficulté* /vu parle avɛk difikylte/, *nous allons à Paris* /nuz alɔ̃ a pari/, *ils arrivent à midi* /ilz ariv a midi/, *il l'a mis au feu* /il la mi o fø/, *venez avec moi* /vəne avɛk mwa/.

19.7.5 Between a noun or adjective and *et* or *ou*, e.g. *les tapis et les rideaux* /le tapi e le rido/, *charmant et intelligent* /ʃarmɑ̃ e ɛ̃tɛliʒɑ̃/, *le sujet ou l'objet* /lə syʒɛ u lɔbʒɛ/, (*est il*) *petit ou grand?* /pəti u grɑ̃/, *étudiants et étudiantes* /etydjɑ̃ e etydjɑ̃:t/, *les Tchèques et les Polonais* /le tʃɛk e le pɔlɔnɛ/, *charmants et intelligents* /ʃarmɑ̃ e ɛ̃tɛliʒɑ̃/, (*est-ce qu'ils sont*) *contents ou pas?* /kɔ̃tɑ̃ u pɑ/. (Some fixed phrases are exceptions, e.g. *arts et métiers* /arz e metje/.)

19.7.6 Between an inverted pronoun subject and any following element, which may be:

   (i) an adjective, e.g. *êtes-vous heureux?* /ɛt vu œrø/, *peut-être étaient-ils intelligents* /pøtɛtr etɛt il ɛ̃tɛliʒɑ̃/

   (ii) a past participle, e.g. *avez-vous entendu?* /ave vu ɑ̃tɑ̃dy/, *sont-ils entrés?* /sɔ̃t il ɑ̃tre/, *peut-être serions-nous invités* /pøtɛtrə sərjɔ̃ nu ɛ̃vite/, *lui a-t-on écrit?* /lɥi a t ɔ̃ ekri/

   (iii) an infinitive (or *y* or *en* + infinitive), e.g. *voulez-vous entrer?* /vule vu ɑ̃tre/, *vont-ils essayer?* /vɔ̃t il eseje/, *voulez-vous y aller?* /vule vu i ale/, *peut-être allons-nous en trouver* /pøtɛtr alɔ̃ nu ɑ̃ truve/

   (iv) a direct or indirect object, e.g. *voulez-vous un bonbon?* /vule vu œ̃ bɔ̃bɔ̃/, *écrivez-vous à Jean?* /ekrive vu ɑ ʒɑ̃/

   (v) an adverb or adverbial phrase, e.g. *en avons-nous assez?*

/ɑ̃n avɔ̃ nu ase/, *viennent-ils ensemble?* /vjɛnt il ɑ̃sɑ̃bl/, *y vont-ils aujourd'hui?* /i vɔ̃t il oʒurdɥi/, *allez-vous à Paris?* /ale vu a pari/, *peut-être viendrez-vous avec nous* /pøtɛtrə vjɛ̃dre vu avɛk nu/.

(The reason for the lack of liaison in this construction, which is one in which foreigners seem particularly liable to use the liaison form – especially perhaps before a past participle, as in (ii) above – is that the pronoun subject is associated grammatically and semantically with its verb, which precedes, and that there is no direct grammatical or semantic link between the pronoun and what follows.)

19.7.7 Between an object pronoun (*nous, vous, les*) post-posed to an imperative and a following element such as an infinitive, e.g. *laissez-les entrer* /lese le ɑ̃tre/, a direct or indirect object, e.g. *envoyez-nous une lettre* /ɑ̃vwaje nu yn lɛtr/, *donnez-les à Jean* /dɔne le a ʒɑ̃/, or an adverb or adverbial phrase, e.g. *asseyez-vous ici* /aseje vu isi/, *laissez-les à la maison* /lese le a la mezɔ̃/.

19.7.8 Between a numeral and the name of a month, e.g. *le deux octobre* /lə dø ɔktɔbr/, *le six août* /lə sis ut/ (*N.B.* the liaison form is /siz/), *le vingt avril* /lə vɛ̃ avril/.

19.7.9 Between an interrogative word or phrase and a verb, e.g. *quand arrivent-ils?* /kɑ̃ arivt il/, *comment écrit-on ce mot?* /kɔmɑ̃ ekrit ɔ̃ sə mo/, *combien avez-vous payé?* /kɔ̃bjɛ̃ ave vu peje/, *quels livres a-t-il achetés?* /kɛl livr at il aʃte/, *lesquels avez-vous choisis?* /lekɛl ave vu ʃwazi/. There are two important exceptions to this, viz. *comment allez-vous?* /kɔmɑ̃t ale vu/, *quand est-ce que* |...|? /kɑ̃t ɛs kə/.

This also applies to an interrogative word and a following word in indirect questions, e.g. (*je ne sais pas*) *comment ils voyagent* /kɔmɑ̃ il vwaja:ʒ/, (*je vais demander*) *quand il va partir* /kɑ̃ il va parti:r/.

20 Intonation

20.1 Introduction

20.1.1 'Intonation' refers to the 'melody' of speech, i.e. to the differences in pitch that occur in speech. When we speak, we do not do so in a monotone: the level of the voice rises and falls according to patterns that characterize the language in question. There may well be considerable differences among regional or social varieties of the same language, and different individuals may use the particular patterns at their disposal in varying ways or to varying extents, but all native-speakers conform more or less to the prevailing practice. Consequently, if a foreigner aims to acquire 'near-native-speaker' proficiency, mastery of the intonation patterns of the target language is essential: even if every vowel and every consonant is perfect, a faulty intonation will betray the foreigner as a foreigner.

20.1.2 The point is made in the introductory chapter to this book (1.1.1) that it is impossible to give, in writing, a fully adequate description of the pronunciation of a language. This is even more true, certainly as far as French is concerned, in the case of intonation than in the case of individual sounds. One reason for this is the complexity and, to some extent, the unpredictability of French intonational patterns. Another reason is that, whereas well established systems of notation exist for transcribing phonemes and allophones of languages with an adequate degree of precision, there are no equally widely recognized conventions for representing intonational patterns. At least four fundamentally different systems, some of them with markedly differing sub-varieties, are in existence and have been used in recent descriptions of French.

20.1.3   The system used in this book is a variation on what is probably both the simplest (in the sense of easiest to grasp) and the most widely used system. It consists of lines printed above each rhythmic group which indicate schematically whether the group in question is pronounced with a rising, a falling, a rising-falling or a level intonation.

It should be noted, that, though the lines representing rising and falling intonational patterns are straight, this does *not* indicate that the intonation of the segments in question rises or falls constantly and regularly from beginning to end. It will be noticed that each line is marked with an arrow. This is intended to suggest that the line indicates the general trend, but only the general trend, of the intonation of a particular segment. In reality, between the beginning and the end of a segment marked as having a generally rising or falling intonation there may well be secondary peaks or dips or short stretches of level intonation, and what is basically a 'falling' segment may well rise a little at the end.

20.1.4   It cannot be stressed too much that all that we aim to present here is as simple an account as possible of the essentials of what is, in reality, a highly intricate system and one which, furthermore, has not yet been fully investigated and analysed in all its finest details. What follows is, therefore, no more than a schematic description of French intonation, characterizing in broad outline the principal intonation patterns associated with different kinds of utterance (statements, questions and commands).

We shall not attempt to deal at any length with the numerous factors that can interfere with these basic patterns.

Foremost among such factors is the expression of any of a wide range of attitudes, reactions and emotions, including surprise, shock, relief, irony, sarcasm, teasing, tenderness, impatience, insistence, anger, caution and authority. To put it in the most general of terms, the effect of such factors is often to cause the peaks or dips in the voice to be somewhat higher or lower than usual, or, when there is emphatic stress, to cause the stressed syllable to be pitched at a higher level than might otherwise be the case. André Malécot sums up the situation neatly when he says (1977: 20) that 'l'intonation est en réalité la somme de plusieurs systèmes superposés, l'un déterminé par la *grammaire*, un autre par les *intentions* du locuteur, un troisième par ses *émotions*, etc.': we, like Malécot himself, shall attempt to cover, and even then only in summary fashion, merely *l'intonation grammaticale*.

20.1.5 The principal intention behind this chapter, then, is to alert the reader to the intonational patterns that occur so that he or she may be in a position to imitate them in an informed way. This is an aspect of French pronunciation where recordings can be particularly useful provided the learner knows what kinds of intonation pattern to listen for.

One further point that must be made is that the foreigner should take care not to exaggerate the patterns and in particular not to adopt too sing-song an intonation by pitching the high points *too* high.

20.2   Types of Utterance

There are basically five types of utterance to be taken into account, viz. (i) *declarative sentences* or *statements* (see 20.3), (ii) *yes-no questions* i.e. questions that can be answered by 'Yes' or 'No' (see 20.4), (iii) *Wh-questions*, i.e. questions introduced by an interrogative word or expression (see 20.5, where the term 'Wh-question' is explained), (iv) *imperative sentences* (see 20.6), and (v) segments of utterances that have a *level intonation* (see 20.7).

20.3 Declarative Sentences

20.3.1 Declarative sentences are those that neither ask a question nor express a command but make a statement. They may be either affirmative (e.g. *Mon frère dit qu'il arrivera demain*) or negative (*Je ne veux pas voir ce film*) – this is of no consequence from the point of view of intonational patterns.

For our present purposes, declarative sentences can be subdivided into three types, according to whether they consist of (i) one rhythmic group (20.3.2), (ii) two rhythmic groups (20.3.3), or (iii) more than two rhythmic groups (20.3.4). They have in common the fact that they all end with a falling intonation. Furthermore, all except those consisting of only one group, and even some of those (see the end of 20.3.2), begin with a rising intonation.

20.3.2 Declarative sentences consisting of no more than two syllables have a falling intonation, i.e. the utterance starts on a relatively high note and ends on a lower one. This does not however mean that each syllable is pitched clearly on a different note (as in singing). Rather, the voice glides down from the higher pitch to the lower. Consequently, a falling intonation can be heard even in the utterances of a single syllable:

J'arrive.   C'est ça.   Bien!

Longer utterances may have a rising-falling intonation, i.e. the pitch first rises to a peak before falling to a lower level at the end of the group. If the first part of the group includes a syllable that could have been stressed (but, of course, by definition, if it is not at the end of a rhythmic group it is not then stressed), that syllable may well represent the peak, e.g.:

Je pars demain.   Mon frère arrive.   Ils viennent tout de suite.

But if no syllable (other than the final one) in a rhythmic group of three or more syllables would be capable of taking a main stress, i.e. if it would not have been possible to divide the group into two, then it is the last syllable but one that represents the peak, e.g.:

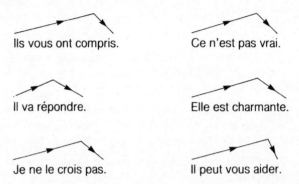

Ils vous ont compris.   Ce n'est pas vrai.

Il va répondre.   Elle est charmante.

Je ne le crois pas.   Il peut vous aider.

(The difference between these and the previous set of examples is that, whereas each utterance in the previous set *could* have been divided into two rhythmic groups, e.g. *Je pars | demain* /ʒə 'pa:r | də'mɛ̃/, it would not be possible so to divide *Il va répondre* and the other examples in this second set.)

20.3.3 Declarative sentences consisting of two rhythmic groups having a rising intonation on the first group and a falling intonation on the second, e.g.:

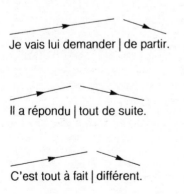

Je vais lui demander | de partir.

Il a répondu | tout de suite.

C'est tout à fait | différent.

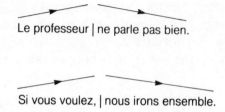

Le professeur | ne parle pas bien.

Si vous voulez, | nous irons ensemble.

20.3.4 In the case of declarative sentences consisting of three or more rhythmic groups, the decisive factor is the point at which the division occurs between the two main parts of the sentence. For example, in the sentence (1) *Je lui ai demandé* (2) *ce qu'il voulait faire,* (3) *mais il n'a pas répondu*, it is clear that this division falls between groups (2) and (3), whereas in (1) *Je lui ai écrit,* (2) *mais il a dit* (3) *que c'était trop tard* it falls between (1) and (2).

Each group in the first part has a rising intonation, and each group in the second part has a falling intonation; the peak is on the final syllable of the last group of the first part, e.g.:

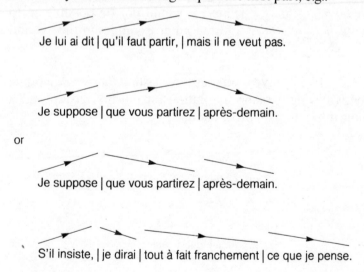

Je lui ai dit | qu'il faut partir, | mais il ne veut pas.

Je suppose | que vous partirez | après-demain.

or

Je suppose | que vous partirez | après-demain.

S'il insiste, | je dirai | tout à fait franchement | ce que je pense.

20.4   Yes-No Questions

Yes-no questions, i.e. questions that can be answered by 'yes' or 'no', have a rising intonation. If there is more than one rhythmic group, each begins on a lower pitch than the end of the previous one, and the peak is reached at the end of the final group. This applies both to questions formed by inversion of the pronoun subject (e.g. *Comprenez-vous?*, *Jean vient-il avec nous?*) and to those in which the word-order is the same as in declarative sentences (e.g. *Vous comprenez? Jean vient avec nous?*). This last type, in which it is only intonation that indicates that the sentence is interrogative and not declarative, is in fact the most widespread form of yes-no question construction in colloquial French. Examples:

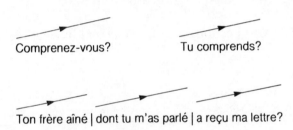

Comprenez-vous?   Tu comprends?

Ton frère aîné | dont tu m'as parlé | a reçu ma lettre?

Note, however, that questions introduced by *est-ce que* may have either a rising or a falling intonation, e.g.:

Est-ce que tu comprends?

Est-ce que tu comprends?

20.5 *Wh*-Questions

20.5.1 *Wh*-questions are those that cannot be answered by 'yes' or 'no' but which include a specific interrogative word or expression enquiring about the identity of the subject or direct or indirect object of the verb (*who?*, (*to*) *whom?*, (*to*) *what?*, *which?*) or about the circumstances surrounding the state, event, action, etc., indicated by the verb, such as time (*when?*, *which day?*, etc.), place (*where?*, *whence?*, *whither?*, *in which drawer?*, etc.), reason (*why?*, *for what reason?*, etc.), manner (*how?*, *in which way?*, *with what weapon?*, etc.). It is because nearly all the interrogative words concerned begin in English with the letters *wh-* that questions of this type have come to be known, sometimes even with reference to languages other than English, as *wh*-questions.

20.5.2 *Wh*-questions are characterized by a falling intonation, e.g.:

Où allez-vous?   Comment se porte-t-elle?

Qui a dit cela?   Que cherche ton père?

If there is more than one rhythmic group, each starts on a higher pitch than the end of the preceding one, e.g.:

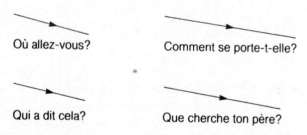

Quand a-t-il acheté | ce dictionnaire?

Pourquoi ton frère | ne vient-il pas?

Dans quelle rue | l'avez-vous acheté?

Note that the same intonational pattern occurs also when the interrogative word is placed (as it frequently is in familiar usage) at the end of the question, e.g.:

Tu pars quand?   Il en a combien?

and in the (strictly speaking ungrammatical but also frequent) construction in which an introductory interrogative word or expression is not followed by inversion of the subject, e.g.:

Pourquoi tu dis ça?   Où vous allez?

A quelle heure | ton frère arrive?

20.6 Imperative Sentences

20.6.1 Sentences including a verb in the imperative (e.g. *Reste! Asseyez-vous! Partons!*) are frequently referred to as commands, but since in very many cases (possibly even a majority of cases) they express not so much a command, in the sense of an order to do something, as an invitation (e.g. *Entrez!*), a request (e.g. *Venez me voir!*), an instruction (e.g. *Allez tout droit*) or a suggestion (e.g. *Prenons une bouteille de vin*), it seems preferable to use the technical term of 'imperative sentence'.

20.6.2   Imperative sentences have a falling intonation, e.g.:

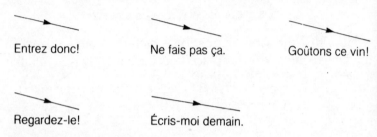

This also applies to the so-called '3rd person imperative' which is expressed by a clause introduced by *que* and having its verb in the subjunctive, e.g.:

20.6.3   In imperative sentences consisting of more than one rhythmic group, the general trend of the intonational pattern is a falling one throughout, but the final syllable of each group except the last one is on a higher pitch, e.g. in:

the voice rises on *dire*, *nous*, *moi* and *frère*.

20.7   Level Intonation

20.7.1   While no type of sentence has a level intonation throughout, a level intonation occurs with certain elements that are, so to speak, inserted in a sentence without forming part of its basic structure. This occurs mainly in relation to (i) parenthetical elements (20.7.2) and (ii) vocative expressions (20.7.3).

20.7.2   Parenthetical comments, 'asides', are often pronounced on a low and generally level tone, though there may be a slight rise in pitch on the last syllable (e.g. *rien* and *-ré* in the following examples):

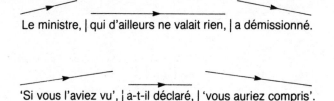

Le ministre, | qui d'ailleurs ne valait rien, | a démissionné.

'Si vous l'aviez vu', | a-t-il déclaré, | 'vous auriez compris'.

20.7.3   Vocative expressions, i.e. names, titles, etc. addressed to the person(s) one is speaking to, and the expressions *s'il te plaît* and *s'il vous plaît*, are normally pronounced with a level intonation at the same pitch as that of the end of the previous rhythmic group. They will therefore have a high intonation if they occur at the division between the two main parts of a declarative sentence (see 20.3.3 and 20.3.4), e.g.:

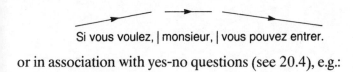

Si vous voulez, | monsieur, | vous pouvez entrer.

or in association with yes-no questions (see 20.4), e.g.:

Tu viens, | Jean-Paul?   Pouvez-vous m'aider, | s'il vous plaît?

and a low intonation at the end of a declarative sentence, e.g.:

Vous pouvez entrer, | monsieur.

or in association with an imperative sentence, e.g.:

Ne fais pas ça, | Jean-Paul.   Écris-moi, | chéri.

References and Further Reading

This list includes only (i) works specifically referred to in this book and (ii) a small number of particularly recommended books on general phonetics or French pronunciation believed to be in print at the time of writing.

Abercrombie, David. 1967. *Elements of General Phonetics*. Edinburgh.

Carton, Fernand. 1974. *Introduction à la phonétique du français*. Paris.

Catford, J. C. 1988. *A Practical Introduction to Phonetics*. Oxford.

Dauzes, Auguste. 1973. *Études sur l'e instable dans le français familier*. Tübingen.

Fouché, Pierre. 1969. *Traité de prononciation française*, 2nd edn. Paris.

Gimson, A. C. 1970. *An Introduction to the Pronunciation of English*, 2nd edn. London.

Malécot, André. 1977. *Introduction à la phonétique française*. The Hague.

Martinet, André and Henriette Walter. 1973. *Dictionnaire de la prononciation française dans son usage réel*. Paris.

O'Connor, J. 1973. *Phonetics*. Harmondsworth.

Tranel, Bernard. 1987. *The Sounds of French*. Cambridge.

Walker, Douglas C. 1984. *The Pronunciation of Canadian French*. Ottawa.

Walter, Henriette. 1977. *La phonologie du français*. Paris.

Walter, Henriette. 1990. 'Une voyelle qui ne veut pas mourir', in John N. Green and Wendy Ayres-Bennett (eds), *Variation and Change in French*, pp. 27–36. London.

Warnant, Léon. 1987. *Dictionnaire de la prononciation française dans sa norme actuelle*. Gembloux.

Index